Voice

of

Her Own

Voice of Her Own

with an introduction by Sherrill Grace

I, Claudia • Kristen Thomson
Dying to be Thin • Linda Carson
Je me souviens • Lorena Gale
Alien Creature • Linda Griffiths
Getting it Straight • Sharon Pollock

Playwrights Canada Press
Toronto • Canada

Playwrights Canada Press
215 Spadina Avenue, Suite 230, Toronto, Ontario CANADA M5T 2C7 416-703-0013
orders@playwrightscanada.com • www.playwrightscanada.com

Playwrights Canada Press acknowledges the support of the taxpayers of Canada and the province of Ontario through The Canada Council for the Arts and the Ontario Arts Council.

The Canada Council for the Arts
Le Conseil des Arts du Canada

ONTARIO ARTS COUNCIL
CONSEIL DES ARTS DE L'ONTARIO

Cover painting "Enigma" by Elaine Heath.
Production Editor/Cover Design: Jodi Armstrong

National Library of Canada Cataloguing in Publication

Voice of her own / compiled by Sherrill Grace and Angela Rebeiro.

Contents: I, Claudia / Kristen Thomson -- Alien creature / Linda Griffiths -- Dying to be thin / Linda Carson -- Je me souviens / Lorena Gale -- Getting it straight / Sharon Pollock.

ISBN 0-88754-662-5

1. Monologues, Canadian (English) 2. Canadian drama (English)--Women authors. I. Grace, Sherrill E., 1944- II. Rebeiro, Angela III. Playwrights Guild of Canada.

PS8309.M6V63 2003   C812'.045089287   C2003-906826-9

First edition: December 2003
Printed and bound by Hignell Printing at Winnipeg, Manitoba, Canada.

TABLE OF CONTENTS

— — • — — • — —

Introduction:

VOICING WOMEN'S EXPERIENCE
by Sherrill Grace

— — • — • — —

"The more women there are making theatre, the more we'll see the
differences between them, the uniqueness of each voice."
—(Cynthia Zimmerman, Playwrighting Women 237)

In the past, when I thought about monologue plays, or plays with long
monologues, I invariably thought of Eugene O'Neill, Samuel Beckett, and John
Gray. Brutus Jones talks to hold his terror at bay, and "Erie" Smith, in *Hughie*, fills
the emptiness of his life by telling stories to a hapless, captive night-clerk in
a hotel; Krapp's existential isolation can only be addressed by a voluble ego
breaking the silence of the void; and Billy Bishop relives his war memories before
us to ask for our understanding, even our admiration, as he struggles to come to
his own kind of terms with his life. In the past, these very different plays seemed
to me to represent what could be done within the limits of the long monologue
form. Such plays, I felt, must be short to sustain interest because they run the
risk of becoming slack, of never finding or creating the tension necessary for
dramatic action. Moreover, such plays make fundamental, unexamined
assumptions about who gets to speak and why an audience (or reader) should care
enough to listen. In the past, I was wary of the long monologue play. I avoided
the form without pausing to ask myself why.

But that changed in 1989, and the play that changed my mind about one-
handers was Wendy Lill's *The Occupation of Heather Rose*. The occasion was a
Fringe Festival; the actor playing Heather was Tamsin Kelsey; the performance
was galvanizing. If theatre can change you, I had been changed. The play worked
so well, in part, because it *moved* – it developed over time and it spoke to me
about things that matter. But it also worked because of Kelsey's bravura
performance; she made me care about Heather; she seized my attention,
addressed me, and didn't let me go. I could (still can) *hear* that voice, that
character Heather Rose telling me her story in ways I simply cannot hear Joey or
Krapp or Billy.

Since *The Occupation of Heather Rose*, I have paid more attention to the long
monologue. What I have discovered, in fact, is a wealth of them,
especially by women, and I am now convinced that long monologue plays by
women, at least in Canada, are something of a phenomenon. They are very good
plays, and I like them.

Of course, to claim that such plays are a phenomenon is to beg several
questions. If more such plays are being written now than in the past, why? If so
many of the best of them in Canada are by women playwrights, why? And how do
these plays work? What can the writer do with, and within, the constraints of the
form? My tentative answers are that these plays are profoundly autobiographical

and that we are living in an age obsessed with autobiography and biography. Moreover, women playwrights have found their voices and dare to tell their stories; they are insisting that their stories matter as much as Krapp's or Billy's, that female experience, insights, knowledge, and perspectives are valuable. Finally, on the question of form, they are experimenting, pushing the limits of the monologue, making it do some amazing things.

Many factors determine what will be selected for a volume like this. Permissions could not be granted for some plays; others have been recently published elsewhere; still others did not seem to be as good *on the page* as in performance, or they did not add to the scope of experience and difference of voice I wanted to represent. Striking absences here are *The Occupation of Heather Rose*, or Joan MacLeod's *Jewel* and *The Shape of a Girl*, but these excellent plays are all easily available in print. The five included here capture some of contemporary women's experiences from childhood to late middle-life; they trace the lineaments of female experience by recreating significant events in a woman's life: the bewilderment and anger of the child who feels abandoned by divorce; the trauma of youth struggling to mirror popular images of how a girl *should* look; the profound dislocations of immigration *within* Canada exacerbated by racism; the dangerous power of creativity in the hands (or mouth) of a gifted mature artist; and the anger of the older woman, with the vision of Cassandra, who dares to take action and is therefore mad. Such a summary of these plays, however, should immediately raise the objection that these experiences are not exclusively female. Which is partly my point. These experiences, if not universal (a suspect word), are every bit as common as those of Jones, Erie, Krapp, or Billy Bishop. What makes these plays so interesting is how well they present their female speakers' experiences and the depth and range of perspectives they represent. Not all these plays could be usefully called *feminist* in any of the term's various meanings, and yet each is firmly situated within the sensibility of a fully present, convincing female speaker. There are no apologies here for this perspective; there is nothing tentative about the way the playwrights seize centre stage for their women.

I, Claudia, written and performed by Kristen Thomson, was a great success in its 2001 premiere at Tarragon Theatre's Extra Space. Claudia, who is twelve, is trying to come to terms with her parents' divorce and her father's remarriage. She is angry, bewildered, and torn between love for her father and loyalty to her mother. To cope, she has withdrawn to the boiler room of her school, where she creates a private theatrical family and an improvised set on which to tell her story. Through Thomson's stunning use of mask and acting skill, her Claudia performs all the roles in this boiler room drama. She is herself, "I, Claudia"; she is Drachman, the school janitor, an immigrant ex-actor and ex-dramaturg; she is Douglas, her father's father; and she is Leslie, her father's new wife. As the masks change, so do the voices, the perspectives, the characters, while underneath them all—all the time—is the child who is desperately trying to make sense of her shattered world by looking at it through four different pairs of eyes. By creating these distinct roles, Thomson has expanded the possibilities of the monologue form while remaining true to the needs of the narrative, which require each character to tell his or her life-story. It is through this telling, this enacting of others' stories, that the child, Claudia, can begin to make some sense of her life. Within this multiple-voiced structure, this psychological ventriloquism, Drachman's position is crucial; he is Claudia's alter-ego; her emotional and creative sounding-board and caretaker. And he is entirely imagined by Claudia. Whatever solace the child finds by the end of her play will come through Drachman's voice and stories, especially his closing fable, which is an allegory of the larger play.

In *Dying to be Thin*, seventeen-year-old Amanda is, quite literally, starving herself in order to reach some commercialized, and internalized, ideal of feminine body-image. She suffers from bulimia, that all-too-common disease in contemporary North American society that afflicts many girls. Structurally, this play is much simpler and more straightforward than *I, Claudia*. Its tone is confessional, and the governing trope is one of confession—to her audience and herself—about what is going on. As she talks to us, she describes her various ruses and self-deceptions. This will be her very last binge, she assures us, as she produces junk food from hiding places in her room. We do not believe her, however, because as she continues her story, she tells us how she has learned to vomit up everything she eats. Portrayed in the locutions of the contemporary teenager, and with the frankness of youth, her description of the bulimic process is graphic and horrifying. Equally disturbing is the rush of words, the volubility that creates the story and, at least while Amanda is still talking, keeps her going, keeps her alive. Her journal (like Claudia's diary) is another verbal refuge through which she tries to convince both herself and us that she can begin a new story, start a new chapter.

Dying to be Thin is closely based on Carson's autobiography and although it is not necessary to know that fact to appreciate the warning and social critique offered by the play, it does remind me of one of the most important motivations for the contemporary use of the monologue form. *Je me souviens* by Lorena Gale comes from the same kind of source – personal memory, deeply felt personal experience. But where the first two plays exist within the tightly closed spaces of the mind (that terrifying place we return to in the last two plays), Gale's play is a work of dramatic expansiveness that reaches across time, place, and physical space to seize our attention. Performed by Gale at its 2002 premiere in Vancouver's Firehall Arts Centre, it brought the full force of the playwright's personal magnetism, energy, wit, bilingual irony, and humour into a face to face encounter with the audience. The play is confrontational; it makes claims and supports them – to identity, nationality, full personhood, and above all to voice and presence. Lorena Gale is who she says she is – "an expatriate anglophone Montréalaise Québecoise exiled in Canada," and living in Vancouver! But it is the way Gale stakes her claim, on stage and page, that makes *Je me souviens* so memorable. At the level of language, the text is rich in image, rhythm, and what I can only call thrust; it moves, leaps, steps back to push further. And it evokes a splendid range of immigrant voices and ideolects that constitute Canadian reality. As performance, the work is a multi-media *tour de force*. In his Foreword to the Talon publication, director John Cooper called this technique Brechtian alienation, but I do not see the play that way. The multi-media—music, film, slides—complement the ventriloquism of Lorena playing, not just Lorena, but the many others who contribute to her memories and thus to her collective sense of self. As we watch her performing her identity and listen to her telling us her story, we are watching how identity *is* performed. For all its theatrics, this is not mere theatre; this is how it is. We all make ourselves up—perform ourselves—as we go along, and we all exist in a complex web of relationships surrounded by, and speaking, multiple voices.

When Gwendolyn MacEwen died at the age of forty-six in 1987, Canada lost one of its finest poets. Very few Canadians, however, paid any attention. MacEwen died alone, an alcoholic, in poverty, and close to starvation. By putting *her* Gwendolyn on stage, Linda Griffiths has reached a larger audience than MacEwen had when she died, and she has brought MacEwen back to life in more ways than one. Of all five plays gathered here, I found this one the most disturbing and haunting in performance, but perhaps that is how it should be; the play, after all, is subtitled "a visitation from Gwendolyn MacEwen." Griffiths has now given us several long monologue plays and she is an outstanding artist in her own right, so when she *appeared* out of the darkness as Gwendolyn I felt indeed that I was in the presence of very powerful magic.

To tell MacEwen's story, or at least parts of it, Griffiths has drawn on MacEwen's work and on Rosemary Sullivan's superb biography, *Shadow Maker* (1995), but as Griffiths explains in her "Playwright's Notes": "She and I are doing this play. Only both of us can speak." Thus, *Alien Creature* exists on that imperceptible boundary that separates yet connects two people. Just as the drama occupies a liminal space between reality and imagination, truth and fiction, presence and absence, so the voice that speaks to us is double – Linda-as-Gwen. This is autobiography-as-biography... and vice-versa. Once we have moved into that liminal space, or been occupied by it, we are ready to hear what the presence has to tell us – straight from the grave, straight from the horse's mouth. In one sense the news is not good: we are gradually destroying all those qualities that make us human—love, beauty, imagination, creativity, art—in favour of an economic and spiritual bottom line; we are starving and impoverishing ourselves and destroying our world. In this respect Griffiths' Gwendolyn is a bit like Margaret Atwood's Susanna Moodie who won't stay buried but comes back to warn us. But the news is not all bad. By coming back to pay this visit, Gwendolyn (Griffiths) proves that the imagination can prevail over "diligent, unimaginative commerce." By coming back to tell us her story, which is ours too, she is telling us she cares. And this is why the play is so haunting. It's not hard to reject bad news, but it is hard to reject someone who fights off death long enough to say – "I want you to know."

In many ways, Griffiths' Gwendolyn is like Sharon Pollock's Eme in *Getting it Straight*. Both *characters* have second sight, wisdom, powerful magic, and both have paid a terrible price for speaking out. If the conformist, unimaginative, forces of society have their way, they will be silenced forever, one by death, the other by institutionalization. For the duration of these plays, however, nothing can stop their speech or deny their presence. The structural *raison d'être* of *Getting it Straight* is actually quite simple – on the pretense of going to the washroom, Eme has escaped her keepers and is hiding under the bleachers at a rodeo ground. From that position she talks to us and to herself. What she tells us, however, and *how* she tells it is anything but simple. In her long, apparently rambling and incoherent monologue, woven from fragments of information about war, genocide, philosophy, literature, popular culture, and classical allusions, she is, in fact, recounting her life story from early childhood to mature married life. And she is confessing. Something has gone very wrong; she seems to have killed her husband, or, at the very least, to have imagined doing so. She is now called mad, schizophrenic, and she has been locked away. What she wants us to know is *why*. Perhaps the simplest answer to this question is that she has taken revenge on a masculine order, represented by the husband, that is threatening to destroy—or has already destroyed in so many wars, in the name of so many ideologies—the world's children and others who are vulnerable. For taking revenge, perhaps just for wanting to, she is now incarcerated. But as Eme (and Pollock) sees it, true madness lies in doing nothing about the destructive rapacity symbolized by the husband and carried, like poison, in his briefcase.

But *Getting it Straight* raises a number of urgent questions that hover over the other plays in this volume, and to these larger questions, the answers are troubling. If, as seems the case, individuals are so threatened by social and economic forces that their survival or sanity is at risk, how can they make a difference or change anything? Claudia cannot heal the wounds created by her parents' breakup; Amanda is so influenced by marketing and guilt that she is on the brink of starvation; Lorena fights hard to smash through the blindness and prejudice surrounding her; and Gwendolyn's voice was ignored, then silenced. That leaves us with Eme, a mad woman, whose chaotic volubility hides a complex story of memory, terror, and rage. If these voices encapsulate female experience in Canada in the latter half of the 20th century, what possible hope is there for any woman to construct her own identity, let alone to prevail upon a society run by men for men (or at least by *some* men for themselves)?

And yet, I think these plays are full of hope. They share an irresistible narrative energy that springs from the power of autobiography; they are telling us stories about personal lives, stories that to some degree we can recognize and share. I would compare them with forms of autobiography such as memoir, testimonial, and confession, and like these forms they promise us secrets, truths, an authenticity and vitality missing in so much of the impersonal, packaged world we inhabit. They also share, and exploit, a crucial sense of connection with the reader (or audience member) because each one is performed for, addressed to us. In their use of the monologue form, they posit an essential intimacy and then go on to make something palpable, uncanny even, out of that connection. For the relatively brief duration of performance or reading, we know we have been touched by another human being. Finally, these five plays offer a beauty of language and a range of performance techniques that stretch and challenge both actor and reader. As long as we can listen to such voices, we will find renewed hope in the efficacy of art, the value of human speech, and the gift of story.

WORKS CITED

— — • — — • — —

Further reading: In addition to the long monologue plays by Lill and MacLeod, see Margaret Hollingsworth's *Diving*, 1983; *Solo*, ed. Jason Sherman. Coach House Press, 1993; *Singular Voices*, ed. Tony Hamill. Playwrights Canada Press, 1997; Guillermo Verdecchia, *Fronteras Americanas*. Talonbooks, 1998; and, of course, Michel Tremblay, *Albertine, in Five Times.* The Talon edition of *Je me souviens* (2001) includes an important personal statement by Lorena Gale, and the Sirocco edition of *Dying to be Thin* (1993) includes an illuminating Afterword with diary excerpts by Linda Carson. For background on *Alien Creature*, see Rosemary Sullivan, *Shadow Maker: The Life of Gwendolyn MacEwen.* Harper Collins, 1995, and Susan Bennett, "Performing Lives: Linda Griffiths and Other Famous Women." *Performing National Identities: International Perspectives on Contemporary Canadian Theatre.* Eds Sherrill Grace and Albert-Reiner Glaap. Talonbooks, 2003. For discussion of *Getting it Straight*, see Cynthia Zimmerman, *Playwrighting Women: Female Voices in English Canada.* Simon & Pierre, 1994. 90-91; Zimmerman's interview with Pollock, "Towards a Better, Fairer World." *CTR* 69 (Winter 1991): 34-38; and Craig Stewart Walker, "Women and Madness: Sharon Pollock's Plays of the Early 1990s." *Sharon Pollock: Essays on Her Works.* Ed Anne Nothof. Guernica, 2000. 128-50. The secondary literature on autobiography is extensive, but see Helen Buss, *Repossessing the World: Reading Memoirs by Contemporary Canadian Women.* Wilfrid Laurier UP, 2002, and Susanna Egan, *Mirror Talk: Genres of Crisis in Contemporary Autobiography.* U of North Carolina P, 1999.

I, Claudia

Kristen Thomson

I, Claudia is **Kristen Thomson**'s first play, for which she received the Arts Toronto 2000 Protégé Honours Award for Performing Arts from Urjo Kareda; and the 2001 Dora Awards for Outstanding Performance and Outstanding New Play. Kristen received a degree in Drama from the University College Drama Program at the University of Toronto and completed the acting program at the National Theatre School of Canada.

I, Claudia was first produced by Tarragon Theatre, Toronto, Ontario in April, 2001 with the following company:

DRACHMAN,
CLAUDIA,
DOUGLAS &
LESLIE   Kristen Thomson

Directed by Chris Abraham
Stage Managed by Shauna Janssen
Set & Costume Design by Julie Fox
Lighting Design by Rebecca Picherack
Sound Editor: John Gzowski

— — • — — • — —

Portions of *I, Claudia* were introduced in Theatre Columbus' Mayhem showcase and then subsequently expanded through Tarragon Spring Arts Fairs in 1999 and 2000. The play then moved to several developmental workshops at Tarragon.

First published in 2003 by Playwrights Canada Press.

Characters

— — • — — • — —

DRACHMAN
CLAUDIA
DOUGLAS
LESLIE

I, Claudia

— — • — — • — —

A red curtain hangs across the space. Drachman enters, pulls back the curtain, revealing the boiler room of an elementary school and in a magical way, reveals a series of placards: "Drachman Presents"; "I, Claudia"; "Starring Claudia"; "And Others". Then Drachman pretends to look for a fifth placard which he can't find, swears in his native language and addresses the audience.

Drachman

Frescia!

Lady and Gentlemen, please to apologize. I was finding a missing placard – and that was a real disgrace because that was my favourite placard to say welcome to each person that was coming here. So now I must to say on behalf of that placard such a welcome to each person really from my heart, such a welcome. Welcome to each person.

As he goes to leave, DRACHMAN pretends to be surprised to find a top hat.

What the hell is this?

He examines it. There is a flash of fire and DRACHMAN magically produces a butterfly from the top hat. The performer then transforms to become CLAUDIA.

Claudia

Ever stare at yourself so hard that your eyes practically start bleeding? I do.

I invited some girls over to my house to work on our science fair topic. Ya, well, most of them didn't want to come. I don't know. I don't live in the same neighbourhood as them anymore so they said it was too far on the subway to get to my house. But I don't think that's true 'cause it only takes me twenty minutes to get home. So I think they might be lying. I don't know maybe their parents are stunned and don't let them go on the subway right, so maybe that's possible. Some parents are very over-protective of their children. And then others, then some others educate their children to be street smart. And I'm street smart. Yeah. I went to a workshop one weekend with my mother. Well she thought it would be a good idea because now I have to take the subway from my house and from my house at my dad's. Some people would say that downtown Toronto is not very safe. But I would not say that at all, right.

I would not say that at all. What I think is if you are someplace where there's nobody there then that's not safe right because there's nobody else to kind of protect you or to see, or to see if you might be in trouble. So that's what I say is not safe. If nobody is there to watch you. Right? So, safety is a very big concern for me. Yeah. Yes, it's a very big concern for me for very sickening reasons because you know, there are vulnerable people in this society, and I am one of them. Like if I lived on a farm, if I was like a farm girl, then maybe it wouldn't be so scary just to be alive. Except I might be afraid of getting my hand severed off by a machine. But I live in a very major urban centre and women and children... which is not to say that, not to say, I mean, I know that there are also racist crimes and there are kinds of crimes against people because of their sexuality and there are also crimes against people like if they are poor. Terrible things happen to poor people. I already know that. I already know that. And I know, I know that I am not poor. Like financially, I'm not very poor at all. Except I'm an only child so I am sibling poor. So, I don't have enough siblings. But I have goldfish. Romeo and Juliet. Two fish, they're really nice and they... I think Romeo might be pregnant. Yeah! Because I got them mixed up. I think that Romeo is a girl and Juliet is a boy! Yeah! I know! But it's hi-larious but it's true. Life is like that sometimes, isn't it? Life is sometimes... sometimes life is so true, it's hi-larious! Don't you find that? So anyway, I think they might be having children, like guppies. Um, is that what you call baby fish? Guppies? And I tell you, that's very satisfying for me. Yeah. And also I want a hamster for my room at my dad's. So cute. Well because in science class we're dissecting frogs, right, so, I don't want a frog because I've already seen one dead. But, but anyways I want a hamster and some gerbils. Something just like, I don't know, just to like enrich my life so I had like a wilderness in both my bedrooms. Like wildlife. Like a eco-system of two apartments and I would be like the migrating bird with two nests, but not like north and south. More like messy and clean. Yeah! My room at my mom's, which is my house, is the messy room. Well, it was the messy room. But my mom said I had to clean it 'cause it was a pigsty with my clothes for carpeting, plus, she said she was going to go through everything with a fine-tooth comb because – now I'm totally embarrassed.

Because I'm going through puberty. Oh my God, I don't even want to talk about it, it's disgusting! Yeah, like oh, oh "you're going through puberty" and everybody thinks they can say things like about if you need a bra or something. It's so embarrassing! It's so disgustingly embarrassing! And you can't even say anything, you can't even say, you can't even say, "STOP IT! STOP IT! STOP IT! STOP TEASING ME!" Right? 'Cause everybody thinks it's so funny and everybody all the grown ups think because they went through it they can just torment you! But they can't. It's totally disgusting and unfair!

As she talks, CLAUDIA gets a snack from her lunch box. She takes out a single man's sock with something in it. She takes a juice box from the sock, sips as she continues to speak, and just tosses the box away carelessly whenever she's finished with it. CLAUDIA should drink as many juice boxes as she wishes throughout the show.

So anyway, because I'm growing, she said she wanted to take a bunch of my stuff that doesn't fit me anymore to the Goodwill and so she said – I had to go through all my stuff, get rid of everything I didn't want anymore and then she said she was gonna go through it all with a fine-tooth comb. My own Private! My own Private Sanctuary or Domain! She was gonna go through it with a Fine-Tooth Comb, that's what she said, you know, exact words, Fine-Tooth Comb!

Well, I had some very private objects in my room that isn't stuff I want to give away and isn't stuff that my mom is allowed to comb through. Like, there were things hidden underneath my bed. Like Evidence and secret objects, and personal musings. Like, essentially the whole stock of my private emotional life which I so can't let my mom see and I so can't put it at my dad's because a lot of it is stuff that I... well, um... I kind of... took... or – as the police would say, stole from his apartment. So I can't really put it there 'cause I only get to see him once a week, so he can't think that I'm, like, his criminal daughter who steals from him.

So I brought it all to the school, down here in the basement, in the boiler room, where nobody goes, except me. Weird and mysterious, eh? Oh, and except the janitor, but he doesn't even wreck it for me, he just leaves me alone. So now this is where I hide my stuff. Men's socks go in here.

She jams the sock into an electric box which is already crammed with socks, and from various hiding spots she produces other objects.

DIARY. Sex book. This very terrible coffee mug. Baggy full of hair. Bunch of other stuff. And, on Tuesday mornings, which is the worst day of my entire life, I even come down here to hide my face.

CLAUDIA changes into DRACHMAN. She may begin speaking before the change is complete.

Drachman

I am finding that girl down here every Tuesday morning. She is very, I'm going to tell you, she is *mitchka* is what we say. She is too young to think on it but hiding this sock in the electric box could cause a very danger. So I am watch always to keep a safety...

He opens the electric box to show how he has sectioned off the interior.

So, you see, I was make this barrier here. And so the sock is separated from the electrical wire, and so. But still, I am watching for her... because she is *mitchka*. Ya? *Mitchka* mean boiling, kind of... *mitchka*... kind of a privacy boiling. Simmer? Is that a privacy boiling? Simmer? But *mitchka* mean that she boil. What a great consequence, yeah? She is *mitchka* in the boiler room. I am tickle to myself on that.

Ah, you see, I am knowing your language! Before I come to Canada, I was translator. Ya? So, I am knowing your language, very details of your language. Example, think on this. In English the word desire is passive word. It's important word, ya? You want, you need, you love – but, you do nothing. Is something else that move you. But, in Bulgonian, that's my language, *udipine* is translate desire. *Udipine*: to lunge, to lurch, to seize upon, to fall like a bleeding monkey on all the bananas! *Udipine* is desire that have the will to possess. When your heart is full of *udipine* you are doing all sort of crazy thing. And that is the Bulgonian way and so, of course, I miss my country, ya? Bulgonia. "Mistress of the Black Sea. He caresses her shores, just above the knee." This is from our national poet, Ungar Bienheim. It is not possible to think on Bulgonia without thinking on Ungar Bienheim. He was carving that nation with his pen. He say: "We are white bears feeding. We are black bears hunting. Great Deer loping. Eagles swooping. Every jagged cliff is my home!"

I am not such an eagle in Canada, yeah? Except this bald head of mine. This hair of mine, I lost it when I was twenty-two. That was my first shit luck. I was actor at this time. It was like, it was like a signal from the theatre god – Drachman, don't act. Nobody want to see a bald leading man. Nobody want to see bald twenty-two year old. Everybody want him off the stage immediately. So, I went from stagecraft acting to kind of translator, yeah? And then became dramaturge. Then, I was... ya...

He catches his reflection and points at it.

...finally that guy right there, he was Artistic Director National Theatre of Bulgonia. It's a comic. I was speaking in images to a mutilated nation and now I am, uh, sweeping your dust bunnies. But, that was my luck. That was my shit luck. And life is like that sometimes, isn't it? Life is sometimes... sometimes life is such a shit luck, it's hilarious. Don't you find that? And, as the famous Bulgonian axiom say: *Ich bat boekin ja wahlieh peitenieh.* The man who is always the same is a stranger to himself. It's a comic. I am used to work in the very best theatre, ya? Very highly-trained performers, very physical performers, very precise physical work. So what, what I'm doing here? Uh? What I'm doing here? Uh? I'm Custodian, ya? Kind of caretaker here at Greenfield Senior Elementary. So, now, ya, I am sweeping the floor, I'm polishing your knob, I am picking this vulgar juice box. But still, I have image and language for my blood and I have my red curtain. Practical the only thing what I was bringing with me from Bulgonia... because I was finding something so magical. I was finding after such a long years on the theatre that if you are simple putting red curtain, all sort of crazy thing have the possibility to happen. All sort of crazy thing.... Like this.

DRACHMAN turns into CLAUDIA who is rocking out.

Claudia

Some kids are mad when they're teenagers, right? Like in movies and at school lots of kids hate their dads. For different reasons at different times. Some kids hate their dad 'cause they want to shoot speed into their arms! Dads don't let them. Dads try to stop them. They say "Fuck off, Dad. Fuck off! I'm shooting speed into my arm and you can't stop me!" And that's 'cause they're into speed.

But I would never do that 'cause I don't hate my dad. My dad is my best friend and I get to see him every week! It starts Monday after school at 3:45. I wait for him in the park across the street from the school and he is never late like other kids' parents and we do something totally bohemian together like go bowling or for pizza. And I have to say, it is the best moment of my entire life because there's so much to talk about and we're both hi-larious. Like every time I say, "I'm thirsty," he says, "I'm Friday," which is just something between us, like father-daughter. And then we go to his apartment which is a downtown condo where I have my own room with a name plate on the door that says "Albert" for a joke and so I say to him, I say, "al-BERT" – and I have lots of posters, no pets, and I do homework and we just hang out and then I go to sleep. And when I wake up on Tuesday morning it is the worst day of my entire life because it's the beginning of the whole next week of not seeing him. So I come down here on Tuesday morning before class to get control of myself.

But Tuesday is also sophisticated because my dad leaves for work before me so I get about twenty minutes in the apartment all by myself, which is a very special time for me which I think of as my teen time. Like, I drink juice but I drink it out of a coffee mug. I look out over the vast cityscape and listen to the top music of my time and, um, okay. Mostly, I do my thing that I do. I take one of my dad's socks from a pair and pack a snack in it, like a juice box, pudding cup, whatever. I just do it for a joke-game to see if he notices that something is missing.... And then I put hair from my mother's brush under my dad's pillow to help them get along. I learned that in voodoo class. And then I... um... well... kind of, um... sneak around to find out information. And there is a lot of information. Look what I found for example six months ago! These! (high heels) I went to my dad next time like, "look what I found by accident. What's? Like whose are these?" And he goes like, fake normal, "Oh those belong to Leslie."

I'm like "WHO?"

"Leslie is a special friend of mine."

Now, I don't want to sound precocious, but I know a euphemism when I hear one. And then, when I finally saw her I KNEW from her boobs how special she was. They were like two flying saucers from another planet that came down and landed on her chest! She came walking into my dad's apartment on a MONDAY night all globbed over in nail polish and lipstick and perfume AND wearing a mink coat with no care for the animals and high heels six feet off the ground! Which are bondage! They are bondage for women! You can get very, you can get very good supportive shoes. My grandmother died from osteoporosis and the bones in her feet like crumbled, they fell apart, and they had big knobs on them so she couldn't even hardly walk and she told me that it was from wearing high heels. So, I'm only twelve-and-three quarters and I already know that. And so Leslie is not very... um... not very... Leslie is... like... stupid.... She says, "Kiddo." She says, "let's you and me be such good friends, and just do girl stuff together, stuff your dad can't do 'cause he's a guy, and we can be such good girlfriends and you can tell me all your problems..."

And I'm like, "Think about it Leslie."

Like, that's just one example of her brain.

I find all my information from sneaking – all the important information about my own life, I find it from sneaking around. Like, I already knew my parents were getting separated from hearing my neighbours through the fence even though they didn't do it until my grandma died. And I already know that my grandpa's giving me my grandma's cameo for my thirteenth birthday. And... I know something else, bonecrushingly agonizing.

Okay. Here's what happened. Stacey and Tracey stopped talking to me again. We were doing our science fair project on rust – just pouring bleach on steel wool and observing it. But then they started ignoring me and passing notes. I was making the pie chart but now they can just shove it. So, then, I wanted to be partners with my best friend, Jojo. She is making a dinosaur out of chicken bones. Her father is an alcoholic on weekends, so she stays with her grandparents on Saturday night. They save the chicken bones and dry them out for her. But Jojo is in a different class, so I wasn't allowed to be partners with her.

And by the way, speaking of alcohol...

She produces a small flask of alcohol that DRACHMAN has sipped from earlier.

Booze. I'm not going to say anything but he could get so fired for that!

So, anyways, you know I have two goldfish, right?

She brings out her goldfish.

Romeo and Juliet and Romeo is pregnant! So, I thought I would have an experiment of observing the new family since I heard that goldfish eat their babies. I didn't even know if that was true, so I went to my mom's office to use the computer but she was on the phone so I eavesdropped. Is that the right word? I listened. I heard her say like " blah blah blah... David's getting married and moving to Brantford. Blah blah blah..."

I'm like WHAT? I didn't even know if that was true. So this morning, at my dad's, I'm just sitting there eating Fruit Loops which I am too old to eat, and when he's just about to go I go, "Congratulations!" He has a cardiac attack. Says he wanted to tell me himself. So I felt really bad about that. Said Leslie wants me for the flower girl. Said Leslie is honoured for me to be the flower girl.

(to goldfish) I bet you never saw a flower girl before. Flower girls never get to say anything. They just have to stand there. They are usually five which is probably old in fish life but it is young in human life. They don't get a statue on the cake. They dress you up like they don't want you to look cool. They want you to look like a loser.

You're not supposed to tap on the fish bowl 'cause it causes a sonic boom for the fish. I was going to take the fish up to class like "Yeah, you have rust, well, I have fish" but then I thought Stacey and Tracey might pour bleach in the water so now I'm keeping them down here where it's safe. So now my topic is like to observe "The Effects of Darkness and Greasiness on Goldfish."

Observation one. Spoke to the fish, no response. Conclusion. They don't speak English. Observation two. Fish grazed the side of the bowl. Conclusion. Swimming in circles.

You know what? If I was a real scientist, I would, I would slap the side of the bowl to discover what the sonic boom really does.

> *CLAUDIA changes into DOUGLAS in silhouette behind the red curtain. He emerges as if looking out the window of his apartment in the early morning.*

Douglas

I can hear those few wee birds just behind the traffic. Lovely. They've been keeping me sane since I moved up here. Big change to move up here. Very big change. I haven't lived alone since my wife passed, Eileen, so I moved up here about a week ago, maybe a few weeks. Yeah. That's right, I moved up here three months ago to be near my son – that's what I was thinking I wanted to say. That's why I moved. To be closer to my son David, my granddaughter Claudia, and his beautiful wife Cynthia. She's a custom-made lady! When those two met, they were so young, it was just like Romeo and Juliet – and now it's all gone to hell. That's right, and now he's mixed up with this new girl, this so-and so. What's her name? Aw, Jesus Christ, what in the hell is her name? Now, I share my birthday with Jesus Christ, so I figure that gives me a pretty good reputation. So for his sake and mine I wish to hell I could remember the name of that girl. Audrey?

> *He begins the long process of unwrapping a candy, speaking throughout.*

Got a weakness for suck candies. Always have. Sweet tooth. That's me. Sweet tooth, sweet toes, sweet heart. My wife, Eileen always said a different part of my body. "Douglas, you've got sweet knuckles." That's from knuckling around in the candy dish, my darling. I have never seen a wrapper so in love with a lozenge. Come loose, you devil. Eureka! We have contact.

So, my son David's coming over with Claudia and that new girl, whatsername? I'm meeting her parents. More in-laws. Told Claudia I'd be her date to the wedding. Meanwhile there's a nice lady down the hall, I was hoping to take her. In any case, I'm going with old Hickory Dickory – that's Claudia. Old Hickory Dickory Dock! That's what I call her. She did the cutest little tap routine when she was... let's see now... five or six years old. There was barely a tap in it. Hickory Dickory Dock, tap, tap – that was it. The mouse ran up the... you know, and then she'd spin around like she was running up the clock. She puts up a fuss, but she'll still do it if I razz her. In any case, they're coming to pick me up at six o'clock. That's about eleven hours away. Got to get an early start. Arthritis. Pain. That's what I say now when people ask, I say, "Don't mind me, I'm just one big pain!" I think Eileen would agree with that, wouldn't you dear?

"Douglas!" That's what she'd holler at me. Endlessly. "Douglas!" But, when she was in hospital, she started calling me Tom. She watched out the window of her room and said she saw fish swimming out there in the parking lot. "Did you feed the fishies, Tommy?" That was her baby brother. Very confused. Very confused. But then right at the end there, she did, she looked right in my eyes, said: "Douglas, who was that pretty girl, Audrey?" Just like it was yesterday. But I never would have remembered that girl's name, not in a million years. Jesus Christ. All those years ago Eileen just showed up at the office. She just came walking into the office with the baby – and I was, I was, I was – mixed up with that girl. But she never said anything about it. She never. Not in all those years... until it was just near the end. I was touching her hair. She didn't have much left. Like a nest of feathers. She looked at me right in the eyes and said "Douglas, who was that pretty girl, Audrey?" I don't know who she was. I don't know. It's better to forget that... that...

That's what I wanted to say. They say that the first sign of going crazy is talking to yourself. Well, not in my case. In my case, it's about the fourth or fifth sign in my case. You hear those stories once you get to a certain age that you accept it and you want to move on? Well, nevertheless, I don't especially want to. I'd like to uh, I'd like to take another spin around the block. I really would. Which puts a nasty thought in my head. You hear that scandal in the papers about the nursing homes where the older people are living? They don't have enough staff, of course, goddamn places never do, and when they're getting too busy they're tying the old people up in the beds. Well, I thought, myself, I wouldn't mind being tied up by a few nurses. That doesn't sound half bad to me. Heavens. I say nonsense like that. You stop me. You stop me before I get started! Because that's the kind of nonsense, I'll say it though. I will. I'll say it.

DRACHMAN appears from behind the curtains and prepares the space for his transformation into LESLIE, using the high heels that CLAUDIA showed us.

Leslie

Come on! Come ON! Pick it up! Pick it up! What's that name tag say? David? Leslie! Come on, you can do better than that, David! Hustle, baby, hustle! You are dancing with the creator of the Regional Supply Network! I don't want to brag but did you come to my seminar? I'm kidding. I'm kidding. I just want to party! I just want to have a helluva good time! That's why they hate me. That's why Michael's over there staring into his dink... I mean his drink!

When I started with the company Michael was my boss. He taught me everything about the company. He put in a lot of extra time with me and it's possible that there was a certain amount of... attraction on his part. I can hardly deny that. But, I'll tell you, he's a Christian and so I never thought it would end up in anything. I mean, I went over to his place for dinner a lot with his wife, Peggy, they've got three, Patty, they've got three lovely kids. They were very, you could tell that they'd been to church, "please" and "thank you" everything. After dinner, Michael would take me through every detail of the company's acquisition and distribution systems, which is where the RSN was born, really. RSN? Regional Supply Network. That's the system I developed! Come on, David, get with the program. Anyway, some nights we'd just sit in the kitchen and I'd spend the whole time just chatting with Peggy... I mean Patty. I was always calling Patty Peggy. I thought she was just going to take my head off.

What? What? Here I am going on about myself. Enough about me, what do you think of me, David? I'm kidding.

Meanwhile, I am dating every conceivable version of Mr. Wrong. I was dating this one guy, so good looking, and he was pretty nice, treated me quite well. And uh, and then he just started acting like a maniac. He drove this big gold jeep. He used to come and park it out front of my building, all night long. Finally I did, I had to call the police – who did nothing. Until I spray-painted "Stalker" on his jeep. Told him if I ever saw his effing jeep again anywhere, I would do the same.

ALL OF WHICH, you see, brought out this over-protective thing in Michael because that's when he started dropping by my apartment. Then the gifts and the notes started. I told him, you know Michael, well, just look at him over there – I said to him, "Michael, you're fantastic, you're the best, you have been so good to me, but you're more like a father or an uncle to me than a" ...yeah. Then he went away. Yeah. After I told him that. I mean he went to Florida. And do you know what I think? I think he went down there and had a few affairs because that's when Peggy Patty left him. And he blames me for that.

Oh yeah! He blames me for her leaving and she blames me for him having the affair! Oh yeah! Welcome to my world, David. That's par for the course. I'm used to it. Everybody! Got a problem? No, I'm serious. Any problems? Blame Leslie! Go for it! Do you have gas? It's probably my fault. Tell me, David, do you ever feel inadequate? 'Cause if you do, you can call me names 'til you feel better.

I don't know why I just said that. I'm kidding. I'm kidding. That doesn't actually happen. But seriously, seriously, it is, it is, it is challenging to be the only woman manager in that office – which is why I am so thrilled, don't tell anybody, I mean, who would you tell, but don't tell anybody. I've been offered a head office posting! Yeah. Brantford. Brampton? Did I say Brantford or Brampton? I always get those two mixed up. It's either Brantford or Brampton. It's Brampton. No, no, it's... where the hell is Brantford, anyway? Do you want to dance?

LESLIE dances into CLAUDIA, leaving her high heels in the space.

Claudia

I'm growing my hair out for my school photos. You know those school photo packages? I'm getting the one with me. Two blow-ups, one for my mom and one for my dad, and then two smaller ones and then six wallet-size photos. One for my mom, one for my dad, one for Jojo, one for Grandpa, one for Leslie, can you believe it? My dad said I have to give her my wallet-size photo and I have to put on the back of it like "LOVE Claudia." Anyway, it's going in my eyes so I've been getting eye infections. Yeah. Like, the grease on the end of my hair goes in my eyes and it makes my eyes get infected. But, right now they're fine. I can see you perfect. Yeah. I think my hair looks pretty good.

Some girls aren't even wearing their uniforms for their picture. Stacey told everybody that she's wearing hot pants and make-up. I might wear bell bottoms and platforms, but not hot pants. I think that they're just too short and my legs would just stick out of them so probably I wouldn't want my legs sticking out like that. Probably not. Especially for the home-room photo where it's not just your face but your whole body plus the whole class plus the home-room teacher, Mrs. Pritchard.

I like Mrs. Pritchard. She's hi-larious. She's so fat, she's sooo funny! She just is laughing all the time. Yeah. She teaches English. She gave us an assignment last week. So hard for the imagination. She said "Use a metaphor to express something about yourself." Like, that's pretty hard, right? Use a metaphor! That's just, like for one thing, I do feel a bit shy about using metaphors and also when you're an official pre-teen like I am, it's considered totally, like, pathetic to express anything about yourself. You're just supposed to act like, duh. Attitude, right? Like, what's an example? Okay. If an old-fashioned type of adult is trying to make friends with you they go, "Oh, what do you want to be when you grow up?" Right? And you should go, you go like this. "I don't know" just shrugging your shoulders, and like all over your face is like, duh. Right? But really the whole time underneath I know I wanna be a DJ or a VJ, 'cause that would rock! That would so rock my universe! Except it might be considered a bit pathetic. Because, like if I said it people might say, like, "How can you be a VJ? You're too ugly." Yeah. That's what people might say to me. But like if I said it I would have to be really cool to be able to say it. So I was just pretending when I said I wanted to be a VJ.

So anyway I tried to write a poem for my assignment, 'cause I like to write poetry. My dad said it's 'cause I'm sensitive. He said it's 'cause I'm sensitive and my mom said it's 'cause I'm emotional. But I couldn't finish it. I wanted to write about butterflies for my own personal reasons and how they start off as basically maggots and then go in a cocoon and then become a miracle but I could only write the first line, like:

You glide, you are throttled through
the black tunnel coming as
a shadow amongst shadows
with urges for light.

But, uh, I got writers block for the rest of that poem. So then I remembered an old dream poem that I wrote before I got my fish, dreaming that I had a sister. Yeah, an older sister. Like a sister who was like a rainbow with many different colours and many different moods and like arching over me to protect me. Just from anything. Just from grey skies. Yeah. But I lost it. Too bad, 'cause that was a very favourite poem of mine. So I had to hand in something, so I handed in one that doesn't make any sense that was very um, unfortunately, that was very uh that was very ugly that's a very ugly nightmarish image called "Black Serpent" with the black serpent that lived in my stomach. And that sometimes got caught in my throat. And I would choke on it and in my poem I would choke on the black serpent but I could never get it out and I would be choking on the black serpent trying to push it out of my stomach, but it would always scoot back down in and lie there just coiled and ready to pounce at the bottom of my stomach. So, I got an A+, higher than Stacey or Tracey. Tracey compared herself to a horse for running cross-country. Duh. But I never showed that poem to my mom and dad even though I got the top grade. No. 'Cause if I showed them, sometimes if I told them that I'm upset or that I am um nightmarish or that I'm choking or that I just feel like sometimes if I said like "uh I'M NOT SO HAPPY AS I PRETEND TO BE!" I think that they would be pretty upset by that. If I just "IT'S A BIG CHARADE" I think that would really upset them. If I said "YOU SHOULDN'T'VE GOT DIVORCED" I think that that would really upset them a lot. And I don't want to cause, like, I always pretend that my mom's just fine, but, I heard her crying. And she's, she's you know we do stuff together but she's not... sometimes I just watch her through the crack in the door. Sometimes I go in and I say "Oh are you okay? Do you want, um, some juice or like a foot massage or anything?" All the curtains are closed even if it's sunny outside. So, my mom is very sensitive.

She is way more sensitive than me even though she's my mom. And my mom is way nicer than anybody else in the world. My mom is smart. My mom is brilliant. My mom is beautiful. And she is way better than anybody else, you know.

So, Leslie is not better than my mom. She is like she is like the crap on the bottom of my mother's shoes. Now, I have to say something nice about her, I know I do. Just a second. What do I like about her?

CLAUDIA puts on LESLIE's high heels and checks out her reflection.

Um... uh... I guess I feel kind of sorry for her in a way because I hate her so much because... I was looking through my dad's wallet and there was just one picture of Leslie in there. Like, the other picture was me and my mom so he couldn't keep that but... I still think he should have my picture in his wallet. But, I can't... "YOU SHOULD HAVE MY PICTURE IN YOUR WALLET." Like I could find another way to say it. A nice way to say it. Plus it's not a good time for causing problems. So, so, I just... I just one day, I just... I just said "oh that's a nice picture. Do you have any other ones?" So that's a different way of saying it – plus I'm getting my pictures done.

CLAUDIA becomes LESLIE in a bridal shop.

Leslie

Hello? Hello? Anyone? How much longer is this going to be? What am I, some kind of second-class citizen? Well, I'm not. And what bothers me, and I don't think I'm acting out of turn here, what bothers me is that I told them I have to get back to work. The dressmaker just turned around and stared at me with a mouthful of pins. He was working on some other girl who arrived at exactly the same time as me. I don't know why they double-booked our fittings, but she has got, I saw her dress, and I don't like it. It has got those big puffy, I don't even know what you call them, those big puffy...

(cell phone) Hello... don't worry, the dressmaker's not here yet. What's up? It'll be gorgeous. Did David call? Oh. Michael? What did he want? Did you tell him I was out of the office? Oh, he can't, can he. What's urgent? He's known about that for two months. At you? What's his number – nine, eight? Five, eight? Thanks.

Admiring her new wedding shoes.

Aren't they sweet?

(cell phone) Michael Oban, please. Michael, don't yell at my secretary... don't yell at my sec.... Don't. No, I'm not talking to you until you agree not to bully my....

Yeah, bully. Bully, yeah... well, keep in mind that yelling is just a louder voice and I can – not until you agree... all right. Oh Michael, you see that's not your department anymore, that's my department.... He doesn't have the trucks or the staff to handle the contra... yeah, 'cause he's your buddy.... It's not my job to keep him in business.... That's not bottom-line thinking... as far as I can tell it's you who can't stop thinking about bottoms, just ask Pegpatty! ...Look, you've known about this for months... I already signed Flatfoot.... You know I mean Fleetfoot.... Well, you also probably think I shouldn't hang up on you right now but apparently I'm such a thoughtless bitch, I think I will... and anyway I'm at a fitting for my wedding dress right now. *(hangs up)*

They think they can just whip it together. Well, it's my wedding dress. It's not, uh, it's my wedding dress, it's not, it's not like uh some small thing. But nothing special can ever happen to Leslie.... That other girl arrived with her mother.

My mother, the only thing she's really focused on is that she wants an organ to play "The Wedding March". But I don't want a traditional wedding in the sense of a traditional wedding. But, that's what she wants. She wants a great whining organ groaning out "The Wedding March". So, I said to David I said, "Well, David, you know, maybe it's not such a bad idea 'cause you know what they say is even more romantic than roses on a piano? Tulips on an organ!" He had to agree with me there!

I love this pearly detail. It's so... just sweet.

Anyway, David doesn't really mind. It's not such a huge thing on David's side. Not that he doesn't care, but with the divorce... so it'll just be Claudia, his father, and a couple of friends on his side. But on my side it will be a huge wedding because, well, it's my first marriage and, oh God, well, I have a bit of a reputation and it probably sounds stupid but I want, I want, I just want everyone I know to see me walk down the aisle with the man I love. That's what I want. And I really want my parents to see that. I want it to be a perfect day and I want to walk down the aisle right past them and give them a little, you know, "fuck you." Like, you didn't think I could do it, well, I did it. Kinda where I'm coming from. I know it was the great joy of your lives to make me feel like an idiot, make Leslie feel like an idiot, the greatest joy of your lives.... Pretty grim, eh?

> *She puts on a wedding veil.*

But somewhere along the line, maybe watching my parents, I don't know, something snapped in my head and went I'm not going to be miserable. I'm not going to be that miserable. I don't wanna be. I just can't be that miserable. And when I met him David was. He was. That's just a sad fact. He just was a totally different guy. He was stiff, arrogant, he had a terrible haircut... I still tease him about it. We were at this conference and I was cutting loose on the dance floor, I was kinda hammered, and I saw him standing there behind his name-tag, handsome... but kind of incarcerated in his suit. You know? Not at ease. So

I just—innocently—grabbed his hand and pulled him onto the dance floor and
he started just kind of tilting from side to side, you should have seen him.
Pathetic. Truly pathetic. But by the end of the night he was covered in sweat,
he had his suit jacket tied around his neck like a cape, I kept calling him Zorro,
and his face was just beaming. So what are you gonna do? I met him at a time
when he was feeling pretty depressed about his life and I know that feeling.
I know that feeling very well. I had to take a little trip to the hospital once
'cause of that feeling. So... we just grabbed each other while the grabbing was
good. And the grabbing was good. And I see him with Claudia and I think,
I want you to be the father of my children too, 'cause I am nuts about her dad.
Kookoo. What's the word I'm looking for? Bonkers? I'm kidding. I love him.
'Cause he's just washing all the pain away... just the regular pain. And when he
looks at me, he sees someone worth loving. Now that's... that's a miracle.

> LESLIE *is wearing the veil and looking at her reflection. She enters into a*
> *fantasy about her wedding. She dances with DRACHMAN's magic top hat as*
> *if with David, finally placing her veil and the top hat in a kind of wedding*
> *portrait. This image lingers as she changes into CLAUDIA.*

Claudia

Romeo and Juliet are dead. Juliet developed a big slimy growth, like infection
on his eye. It was all long and white and trailing off his eye. And flowing around
in the water. He looked like Leslie in her white wedding veil just trailing off
her head like an infection 'cause they got married on Saturday. It wasn't even
magical. And on Sunday the fish died. Juliet didn't even seem to notice the
infection even though in such a small, cloudy fish bowl you think you would
go mentally insane with such a big, long infection.

Too much fungus. That's what my mom said – from over-feeding. But feeding
fish is practically the only thing you can do with them – especially to observe
them scientifically. Otherwise they are just swimming. And what's swimming?
It's not science! So, I kept sprinkling and sprinkling and sprinkling and
sprinkling and sprinkling food in the water – until I became a murderess.
And then guess what I found out fish food is made of? Crushed butterflies.
Each little flake is a dried, crushed butterfly wing. So I'm writing one eulogy
for everybody before flushing:

Fish to water, Wings to air.
Farewell to all that's gold and rare.

And when I'm finished I guess I'll just flush them.... And then yesterday, my
science fair project was due. My class was supposed to set up our display tables
in the gym but I just went home. I didn't even go to my dad's even though it
was Monday 'cause he left on Sunday for his honeymoon in Italy. And today,
it's Tuesday, so I wonder what's special about today? Armageddon? Just joking.
I know what's special. It's a very special day.

Remember I said my grandpa was giving me my grandma's cameo for my thirteenth birthday? Well, what do you call this? That's my grandma when she was young. And who is wearing new platform shoes, even though my grandma wouldn't like it and even though my mom always swore no way, no way, no way, she would never buy me high shoes, high shoes are bad for growing feet but then she still bought me my dream shoes! Rock!

The shoes look like a child's version of LESLIE's shoes.

My dad gave me a million dollars to buy whatever I want. Just joking. He gave me two hundred dollars, though – one hundred for graduating and one hundred for my birthday! And… the guy who's the janitor, he has the wizard face. He doesn't even have a very nice face. Some kids think he's scary but I don't. I saw him through a crack in the door. He pointed over there, said like "Ja, Jaaa" and closed the door behind him so quiet like a total librarian. Too bad he doesn't even speak very much English, we don't even speak the same language, except this note which I found: "Miss. A minor token for your commencement. Sincere Regards, Drachman, The Caretaker." And there was this.

The top hat. She looks inside and reads.

Made in Bulgonia. Weird, eh. I guess when you're a teenager, everybody can tell. When you're thirteen, even if you don't graduate into high school, still, you are, you are commencing on getting much needed guts and a subversive attitude towards the status quo.

Example. Science fair is going in the gym right now and I'm skipping 'cause I already know I'm going to fail. I already know that. So why should I pretend I learned something? And anyway that would be lying because I didn't learn anything. I just made a bunch of fake diagrams. Like this thing. This I did one day to show the pattern of the fish swimming in the bowl. What does it mean? I have no idea!

She tears the diagram.

So. Screw the science fair. So? Screw the wedding. Yup.

Stupid sucks, sucks so bad, that wedding sucked so bad. 'Cause I went to that wedding with my grandfather. I was just wearing sweat pants, I was just wearing crap pants to go and pick up my grandfather, 'cause I was supposed to get into my you-know-what dress. I had to go over to Leslie's with her and all the bride maids and I had to spend time with her and not with my even dad even though it was more a special day of his and also it was practically my birthday-eve. I hated that day so bad. And that's why it makes me so mad and that's why I'm not going to talk anymore. And I already told them that. I was mad like a teenager gets mad. On any movies that I like now there's always a teenager that gets really mad and goes into rebellion fits and I was like a total rebellion fit. So you know what I did? Um, I had a public rebellion fit. Because I was putting this dress – if you could have seen this thing – on the back it had a big bow almost as big as my whole bum, the whole bow. They even took a picture of me in it. And then there was also, like, uh, a carousel flower circling around my head. I took one look at myself–

And that's when I started screaming. I was! I was screaming like a maniac.

"STOP THE PROCEEDINGS! I DEFY YOU STARS! NOBODY ASKED MY PERMISSION!"

Can you imagine such pureness in front of everybody? Staring at the congregation, shaking in my boots, knowing I wrecked everything. Wrecked it! Wrecked it! Wrecked it! Wrecked it! Wrecked it! Wrecked it! Wrecked it! Wrecked it! Wrecked it! Wrecked it!

Standing there with a needle in my hand "WHO'S GONNA BE THE WISE GUY WHO ASKS MY PERMISSION OR I'M GONNA SHOOT SPEED INTO MY ARM AND THEN I'M GONNA SNORT," like what do you do with crack cocaine? "DO SOMETHING WITH CRACK COCAINE TO MAKE ME ADDICTED FOR LIFE AAAAND IF I'M SO ADDICTED I MIGHT END UP, I might end up killing myself."

The groom comes under a cardiac attack. Very serious. Drags me back to the vespers, like the quiet church place, whispering but screaming: "Why you little brat. How could you ruin this day?"

And then I go like, "Ooooh yea, well, how come you ruined my life? Now you only want to see me one Monday and now you want to move even further in a different city."

He's like, "Blah, blah, blah... Leslie lives in Brantford, Leslie is my wife, I love Leslie, Leslie, Leslie, Leslie, blah, blah, blah..."

"Oh, you precious you are in love and now you get to do whatever only you want and I am the garbage kid that you can throw away in the garbage can of life!"

He's says I'm old enough to understand. "YES! I am old enough to understand. So why don't I? Whose fault is that? Maybe yours 'cause of what I found out."

Don't tell my mom.

That this conference coffee mug that I stole from my dad's apartment actually belongs to Leslie. I thought it was my dad's because it's from a conference he goes to every year. But Leslie told me that it was hers. She said she went to the same conference as my dad. The date on this coffee mug is 1997. But my mom and dad didn't separate until Grandma died in 1999. "So you didn't split up because you were unhappy but because you were a little too happy with other people at a conference in 1997 when we were still a family."

Silence. Silence on the vespers. Okay.

He says that life is very complicated and that sometimes people don't mean to but sometimes people fail each other.

I said, "Yeah, you did fail. So I need some time to figure things out so I need to wear my own outfits for a while and not be the flower girl."

And he said, he said, "You're right. You are not going to be the flower girl, you are going to be the best man. I have a tuxedo rented for you in the back. Go put it on and we'll walk down the aisle together, pal. My darling, my love."

I said: "Really? Do you really mean it?"

He said: "Yeah, I really, really mean it."

And I said: "Is there a top hat?"

And he said: "Yeah, there's a top hat."

And so I went and put on my tuxedo and my top hat and even though I can't dance I did a soft shoe routine at the reception. And everybody laughed. And even my mom was there, she was, laughing and totally amazed 'cause everybody thought I was just gonna do Hickory Dickory Dock, but I did Fred Astaire. "Singin' in the Rain."

That really happened, you know. In my mind, I didn't wear that dress. In my mind...

Like, it's not even so much, like sometimes, I don't even know why I think it's my fault. I don't even know why. Like, sometimes the only thing I could think of is that my dad thought I was just too ugly. Maybe that's why he left... but that doesn't make any sense... but maybe I'm a butterfly. Maybe I'm just in my cocoon right now. Maybe nobody thought of that but maybe I am. And maybe I will get better so that they, so that my mom and dad think that if I was good enough they better stick together to be my parents, right, 'cause I'm a really good kid. Has to have their parents, right? There's, there's, there's...

Unable to continue speaking, CLAUDIA becomes DRACHMAN.

Drachman

DRACHMAN mops the floor as he talks. At the end the floor should be like a glimmering pool, reflecting the set, the lights of the theatre, etc.

To conclude, I would like to tell to you famous Bulgonian fable, very short story, that my mother was telling to me when I was crying and so I was telling to my son, and so of course this story I am loving it very much. Yeah, I have a son, twenty-two, he is live in United State – but we are not talking on that.

Once upon a time, in a land as close as your thoughts, a naughty little spragnome was climbing through the window of a tiny straw hut and peek into the cradle of a newborn baby and whisper to her sleeping parents this promise. "Weave this child a basket to contain all what her heart desires and when it is full, I will return to make her wise." Now, I must stop to tell you that in Bulgonia we know this spragnome very well. He is very tiny, like my thumb, particular type of gnome which seem to do one thing, but always he is doing something else. So, to continue. Next morning, the farmer is cutting the straw and his wife is weaving that basket and for many years that child she take her basket and she go in her life gathering, gathering, gathering everything that her little heart want. Until her basket is so full. And when it's so full she have to put it down. Now, it's too heavy. Even so much pleasure, ya, it's not possible to carry on endlessly. You know. So she put her basket and so she go and she have a little sleep, something, and when she wake up she come back to find that her basket was complete empty! How did this happen? Well, on this moment, after such a long years, that naughty little spragnome is appear to make her wise! She point on that crazy midget yelling "Thief!" And she begin to search on him and searching on every place until she see that she cannot find not one thing, not one hope remaining. All is gone. And so, she collapse on her basket and begin weeping, "Now I have nothing left but my sadness." And so she cry and she keep to cry until practical flood of tears was filling her basket. And when her basket is complete full of tears that spragnome point. He say: "Now, you see, your basket is no longer empty. Now it have very much inside. Lugaldya. Look." And when she look she saw that her basket was become a deep pool… brimming with her experience and dancing on the surface of her tears… yes, very clearly she perceived it. Reflected on the surface of her grief she saw herself.

    DRACHMAN closes the red curtain.

    The end.

Dying to be Thin

Linda A. Carson

Linda A. Carson, a graduate of Vancouver's Studio 58, has been a professional actor, clown, and writer for the past 16 years. She has acted in theatres across Canada, and performed her clown characters at International Festivals. Upon graduation from theatre school, Linda wrote and toured her one person play *Dying To Be Thin*, and won the Jessie Richardson Award for Emerging Playwright. Linda's next play, *Mom's The Word*, which she co-created and toured with five other actor/writers, won the Jessie Richardson Awards for Best Play and Best Ensemble Cast. Linda's latest credits include acting in Carousel Player's production of *The Last Drop*, by Kim Selody, and being nominated for a Dora Award in Carousel Player's production of *Patty's Cake* by Tim Webb. Linda has recently moved with her family from British Columbia to Ontario where she continues to write and act.

Dying to be Thin was first produced by Carousel Theatre, Vancouver, British Columbia in November, 1992, with the following company:

AMANDA Jones   Linda A. Carson

Directed by Pam Johnson
Set design by Douglas Welch
Stage Manager: Eileen Stanley
Production Manager: Bruce Watson
Sound design: Greg Sawka
Props construction: Valerie Arntzen

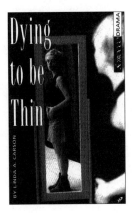

First published in 1993 by Scirocco Drama, an imprint of J. Gordon Shillingford Publishing Inc. Reprinted with permission.

Characters
— — • — — • — —

AMANDA Jones (17)

Time
— — • — — • — —

The present.

Setting
— — • — — • — —

AMANDA's bedroom. Occasionally the script will mention items like a bed or chest of drawers but these are not necessary and can be substituted. There does need to be some sort of table, a place or places to hide food, a working toaster oven, a wall or bulletin board, and something to represent a toilet.

Dying to be Thin

— — • — — • — —

Act One

*It is morning. AMANDA is lying on her bed asleep. She is dressed in her
dressing gown. There are half eaten bits of junk food all around her spilling out
of a paper bag. A tape quietly begins to drone: "chocolate, icing, cookies, bread,
sugar, butter, cake, chocolate, icing, cookies, bread, sugar, etc." She wakes and
looks at the leftovers. She feels sick. She listens to the drone; as if the words are
the thoughts in her head. Heaving herself up, she walks to the bathroom. She
looks at herself in a mirror, questioning silently why this person would eat so
much. She then turns to the toilet. She takes a deep breath as the "drone" fades
into the sound of constant toilet flushing. AMANDA begins to throw up a
coloured, magician's streamer, called a mouth coil, from her mouth. Finishing, she
stands up and breathes a sigh of relief. The mirror reflects back to her a cleansed,
more positive person, fresh for a new start. She leaves her bathroom, but as she
does, she discovers the audience staring at her. Acknowledging them, she realizes
that she has been caught. As the play continues she talks directly to the audience.*

AMANDA

You, just saw that... *(She makes an excuse.)* I couldn't help it. I've got the flu...

*She remembers the spilled leftovers and goes to hide them in the paper bag but
stops, realizing it is too late. She turns back to the audience and ensures them
emphatically.*

That was my last time.

She goes over to her desk and pulls out her journal. She writes:

"A New Beginning."

She stops and decides to confide in the people watching her.

I've had so many "New Beginnings." Maybe I'm addicted to "New Beginnings"
and that's why I keep on wrecking them. I am sick of messing up!

She leafs through the journal.

I blew it here – and here – and here – here, here, and... I'd die if anybody
I actually knew ever found out.

She pauses and is suddenly hit by a thought.

What if I did die? What if—somehow—I ceased to exist and my Mom and Dad – or my friends read this? Woe!

She quickly rips out the previous pages of her journal and destroys them.

No way! No, no, no way!

There is not much of the journal left. After considering it, she throws away the whole book and digs out a brand new journal. She continues with conviction.

This book shall only contain perfection.

She titles it.

"Amanda Jones." That's me. "My Success Journal."

AMANDA closes the book and swears on it.

From now on, everything I write in this diary will be a record of my success. "White Rabbits, White Rabbits, White Rabbits."

That's what my Grandmother used to say on the first day of every month. She said it brought her a present but I use it for good luck.

AMANDA is reminded of her grandmother's ring and pulls out a special box.

This is my Grandmother's ring.

She opens the box.

She gave it to me last year just before she died. I swore that when it was on my finger, my hand would stay away from all junk food, but I kept on messing up so I put it away until I had smartened up.

"I hereby vow, on my Grandmother's ring, that I will be perfect from now on."

She ceremoniously puts on the ring

Because... "diamonds are forever! And today is the first day of the rest of... forever!" I just have...
Twelve hours ahead,
A safe pathway I'll tread,
Before I'm safely back to bed,
Perfect living, all day long,
Surroundeth me!"

She finishes with one more, very serious vow.

If I ever wreck my diet again – this ring gets flushed down the toilet.

> *AMANDA pauses and wonders what to do next. She looks around her room until she catches her image in the mirror. Her spirits slip a little as she looks at herself and she goes over to the scales. She takes off her dressing gown and carefully steps on. They give her worse news than the mirror and she gets off defeated. She remembers her vows and rallies herself onward.*

Okay, okay, I just need to find a new diet.

> *She goes to a large pad of paper hanging up in her room and pulls down an old diet plan. She begins working on a new one. She writes in big letters:*

"To lose! Ten pounds!"

> *Finishing, she imagines herself already there.*

You know, right now, if I was ten pounds less? I'd be dressed in those jeans...

> *She points to a tiny pair of jeans and a small, fashionable top hung up on display.*

...with my perfect belt, and my new top – and I'd have my homework easily done and slung over my shoulder as I breezed out that door to meet Robbie, he's my boyfriend, and we'd go and shoot some baskets or something, and then he'd walk me to my locker, and my friends would gather round and we'd all go into class, laughing.

> *AMANDA catches sight of herself in the mirror and is brought back to reality. She covers herself up in her dressing gown again.*

If! If I was ten pounds less!

> *AMANDA sees a picture of her sister.*

My sister is! This is a picture of her she sent to me from her university.

> *She reads the back of the picture.*

"Dear Amanda, I hope you're felling better and that your new diet is going well." We used to diet together. "As you can see I finally managed to lose that last eight pounds and I'm *so* much happier and I'm having *so* much fun. But I'll be home next weekend so we can catch up. Love, April." I can't stand the thought of my sister seeing me like this!

> *Her spirits have slipped even further but then she suddenly gets excited.*

Maybe this is just what I need! April coming home will make me really stick to a diet! I'll make up a "Sister Coming Home Plan!" One that will get me skinny by the time that she gets here!

AMANDA madly begins to look through a pile of magazines and diet books. She comes across a lovely dessert and shows it to the audience.

You know, sometimes when I try to diet, all that comes into my mind are pictures of these terribly fattening foods. And it happens when I eat too. I go to eat something that's good for me, like an apple or a carrot, and the next thing I know I am cleaning out the whole fridge. Eating's the problem! If I didn't have to eat—anything—ever—I'd be fine!

She suddenly gets an idea.

That's it! I won't eat! I won't eat until my sister comes home!

AMANDA goes over to her hanging paper and writes.

"Eat Zero Calories."

Very pleased, on top of the world again, she starts to get dressed while figuring out the logistics of her new plan.

It will be tricky with Mom and Dad. There's no way they'd let me do it. No way! My Mom swears by the Jenny Craig diet, and my Dad – he thinks maybe if I just don't eat between meals. So I'll have to pretend that everything is fine and I just can't make it home for dinner. I'll say, "there's this big volleyball tournament coming up so we have to practice," but instead I'll just go for a jog by myself. Jogging! That's a great idea!

AMANDA goes back to her plan and writes:

"Jog! One Hour Per Night." This way I'll burn up seven hundred and eighty more calories besides the zero I've eaten! I bet I'll lose more than ten pounds!

AMANDA surveys her plan happily and decides to add: "Starting Weight." She then goes over to the scales and carefully gets on.

I weigh myself a lot. Probably – well, at least 24 times a day. If I'm on a diet I like to see the weight go down, and if I'm not, I've got to make sure the fat doesn't sneak back on – which it does! It's best not to wear anything at all though because every little bit adds up. I used to make myself strip down to nothing every time, but that was hard so then I weighed all my clothes, and now I just subtract them from the total.

AMANDA does a calculation and writes her weight up on the paper. If she wants she can add a heading: "End Weight" for inspiration, and draw a graph line down to her ideal weight of one hundred and five pounds.

You should never use those big doctors scales, no way! They're good for an instant five pound gain! I always use the cheapest scales going.

AMANDA displays her scales and demonstrates with them.

The cheaper the scales, the less you weigh, especially if you put them on a carpet! And I never jump on. I hold on to something and ease my weight on bit, by bit, by bit, so it ends up at the lightest weight possible.

AMANDA has held onto her table and is taking her fingers off one by one.

And if I'm not happy with that, I set the little marker to just below zero, and as long as I come off the scales super slowly too, it ends up back on zero so I can believe the weight I just saw!

She puts the scales back to their original spot.

It won't be long before I'm back in this bed tonight and I am soooo happy that I made it through my day, and I am soooo happy that I am skinnier!

She relaxes into the happy thought but then sees her leftover junk food and jumps back into her planning mode.

I've got to get these out of the house so nothing tempts me! You know, it'll be easier if I get *me* out of the house. The safest place is at school – but I hate anyone seeing me like this. Never mind, it's for the best and it won't be for long.

AMANDA makes a phone call. She has a phone with a monitor. We can hear Robbie's voice on a recorded message.

"Hi, Robbie here! SSSZZZZZZZZZZ. If it's before 8:55, I'm not up yet! Snorrrrrrre! But talk to me anyway and I'll get back to you."

AMANDA leaves her message.

"Hi, Robbie? It's me – uh – listen, sorry I didn't get back to you all week, I, uh, had this really bad flu – but I'm feeling way better today so I thought I'd come to school and maybe you could meet me at my locker and I could give you back your math notes and we could talk – and stuff. Listen, Robbie, my face is still really fat and swollen from being sick, I hope you don't mind.... Anyway, I'll see you in forty-five minutes. Oh, it's me, Amanda."

AMANDA hangs up the phone and gets herself ready for school.

My friends must think it's weird the way I'm sick so much. I used to do everything with them but now I'm always waiting until I'm skinnier before I let myself go out. Even Robbie's almost given up on me. We've been going out for about a year now. We run together, snowboard, play basketball, volleyball... except this year I didn't try out for volleyball because I looked way too fat in my shorts. I got so depressed I blew it for a week.

>*Ready for school, AMANDA gets the bag of leftovers and goes to leave but is stopped by a note slipped half way under her door. She picks it up.*

"My dear Mandy, I didn't want to disturb you this morning as I heard you up studying well past midnight." I wasn't exactly studying. "Here is a snack to pop in your bag to feed your mind! We'll see you for dinner. Love, Mom."

>*AMANDA discovers some rice cakes left by her mother. She looks at them and then crumples up the note. Her spirits have slipped.*

Doesn't she know that it's dangerous to let anything into your mouth when you first start out on a diet because you always end up wanting more?

>*She looks at the rice cakes.*

The trouble is I am awfully hungry. I sort of haven't let anything stay down since – the day before yesterday. It's probably stupid to try to start off a fast already hungry. Maybe I should have one – to make up for yesterday. I mean, one rice cake in seven days isn't going to hurt anything! Okay, Mom, I'll have one.

>*AMANDA takes out a cracker and goes to eat it.*

You know, since this is my last meal, I might as well enjoy it.

>*She goes to retrieve some peanut butter from a hidden spot.*

Peanut butter. It's good protein. It will feed my mind!

>*She finds a hidden knife and spreads peanut butter on the rice cracker. As she finishes she gets another idea.*

And you know what else? This will be delicious!

>*She dives to another hidden spot.*

Chocolate sauce!

>*She takes a moment to justify it.*

That will take care of my chocolate cravings for the seven days too!

>*She scoops on chocolate sauce. Her spirits have picked up again.*

It looks like a giant Reese's Pieces! Except it needs a little colour – I have just the thing!

She gets some hidden Smarties.

Smarties! "When you eat your Smarties do you eat the red ones last? Do you suck them very slowly, or crunch them very fast!"

> *She covers the rice cracker with Smarties and takes a big bite, enjoying it. She takes another bite but suddenly stops and looks at the smothered piece of food.*

What am I doing?

> *AMANDA drops the cracker.*

Stupid! Stupid fat me! Some first fast! Why didn't I just get out of the house? Stupid Mom! I wish she'd just mind her own business! I'm such an idiot! How am I supposed to lose ten pounds now in time for my stupid sister coming home?

> *She jumps on to scales.*

I'm already up a good five!

> *AMANDA eyes the gooey rice cracker.*

There's no way I can let *that* stay down.

> *She continues, defeated.*

I should have got rid of those Smarties last night – and that, and that...

> *She indicates the other food on the table.*

I need to get rid of it all so it doesn't come sneaking up on me.

> *AMANDA pauses as an idea dawns on her.*

Well, maybe that's it!

> *She begins to plan.*

Since I have to throw up anyway – I could get rid of all my cravings and all this food at once! I could have this huge feast – of everything I've ever wanted to eat so that I'll never crave again! I can't believe I haven't thought of this before! I will have my, "Last Ever in My Whole Life Binge!"

AMANDA is feeling more and more excited. She retrieves her bag of leftovers that she was going to throw out.

It'll be good not to waste these!

She reaches into the bag and pulls out one or two half-eaten items and then stops as she finds some sliced, white Wonder Bread.

This, I love! Wonder Bread! When we were little we used to make it up into little dough balls.

She squishes some up into a little ball.

It would taste just like home-made bread.

She eats it.

Mmm, dough-dough bread!

During the following section each time she mentions a food it gets retrieved from a hidden spot in her room and put on the table.

And these!

She has suddenly remembered another one of her favourites.

Paydirt!

She presents a package of crumpets to the audience.

Ta da! Crumpets! We used to always have them for special occasions, like birthdays or Christmas. Delicious...

She pulls out a toaster and plugs it in.

...toasted! Nobody knows I have this! I have to be careful when I use it because of the smell. And they'll have to have butter, dripping off them.

She pulls out some margarine.

I use this because it's cheaper – and sugar, and cinnamon! It's like a fresh, hot, cinnamon bun! I love cinnamon buns. I have a cinnamon bun!

She digs out a half-eaten cinnamon bun from her bag of leftovers.

Oh, and since this is "The Last Time," I'll have to have my favourite!

She gets out a bag of icing sugar.

Icing!

> *AMANDA finds a bowl and a spoon and begins to cream the icing sugar with the margarine.*

If Mom ever made a cake, my sister and I used to wait around for the beaters to lick. I'd lick each metal spoke over and over but I never seemed to get enough.

> *She casually gets some milk from the back of the toilet or another hidden spot.*

Now I never let myself touch the stuff because I know it will turn into instant fat.

> *She quietly mixes up the icing for a minute and then looks around for something to nibble on.*

When I am busy getting stuff ready, I like to have a little something to tide me over.

> *AMANDA continues to look around the table of food and stops at the bread.*

Sugar and butter on white bread is perfect, because it's fast...

> *She butters and sugars a piece of bread and takes a bite.*

...and delicious. Or cookies! Cookies are great tide-me-overs!

> *AMANDA finds a bag of cookies.*

You can open them up on the way back from the store.

> *She opens them and spreads a few on the table.*

They're getting expensive though. But sometimes you can find rolls of cheap ones in the drug store.

I go shopping a lot. Sometimes to quickly replace the food I've eaten from the cupboards, or sometimes for direct supplies. It gets expensive! I bet I spend...

> *She pauses to calculate.*

...over a hundred dollars a week. I spend all my clothing allowance, any money I get from baby-sitting – I've even spent most of the money I got from my Grandmother. And it gets embarrassing when I have to unload it all, in front of everyone, at the check-out! I usually go to different corner stores so nobody will remember me, and I'll make up stories like – that I work at a day care and we're having a birthday party or something. And I always ask for paper bags.

I hate using plastic because if I accidentally meet someone they might see what's inside.

AMANDA takes the bread and spreads each piece with icing, making a stack of six to eight slices.

For a binge that I have lots of time for, I like to get a huge pile of stuff ready so I can plow into it nonstop.

She finishes.

There.

She picks up the stack and shows it to the audience.

This isn't much at all. Usually I can eat three times this amount, but today, for my last time, I get variety...

AMANDA puts down the bread and goes to get something else.

...like, why not, taco chips! They are hard to bring back up though, they come up in big lumps... but what helps that is popcorn! It sort of gathers everything up on it's way out.

AMANDA surveys the feast and remembers one last thing.

Crumpets!

The crumpets have popped out of the toaster. AMANDA lathers them with butter, cinnamon and icing sugar. She takes a delicious and most satisfying bite. She looks out at the audience and enjoys the crumpet with them. She takes another bite but becomes painfully aware of the audience staring at her. She surveys the food table and tries to take another bite of the crumpet. She stops. The grossness, the strangeness, and the shamefulness of what she is doing, in front of them all, hits home to her. She moves away from the food.

AMANDA quietly tries to explain.

I don't know why I do this. I don't know... I mean... this me? This me that's talking to you right now? I would never do that. I mean – I'm sane – I'm intelligent – and I have this great life – and *I* would never waste my time doing that.

She pauses to try and figure it all out.

It seems like – this other thing possesses me, out of the blue – and I end up doing it – and *this* me gets smaller and smaller until it almost goes away. But it never actually does. There's always a little part of it left, right back here.

She indicates a specific place at the back of her head.

And if I look at the world outside, it seems like there is this thick glass or haze separating me from it. Or if I look at people around me, they seem really really far off, like in another space. And while I eat, this tiny part of me watches, and sometimes tries to make me stop, but it can't, because it's way too small so I just block it out. That way I can finish eating and throw up. Throwing up is the only route back to *this* me.

AMANDA looks back at all the food.

After the initial relief of deciding to eat and the fun of the first few bites, I don't like to think about it – or even look at it. So I'll do something else like, I'll watch TV while I eat, or I'll read something.

AMANDA glances over at her pile of magazines.

In fact, I was eating and reading a magazine when I found out what this whole thing was! I couldn't believe it! Up until then I had honestly thought I was the only one in all the world that would do such a weird thing! I thought I'd been directly reincarnated from the Roman times or something, when they used feathers to tickle their throats! And that's when I found out what it was called "Bulimia." Right away I hated that word.

She repeats it distastefully.

"Bullliiimia." I still hate it! Why did they have to call it that? Bul – bul – it sounds like they are making a stupid joke about regurgitating cud – or it sounds like the name of a huge fat cow...

She demonstrates.

"Bulimia," with these giant udders that flop from side to side – it's ugly, dumb, it sounds fat!

AMANDA shudders.

I could never imagine going to anyone, not even a counsellor and saying, "I have Bull-iii-mia." That would be so awful.

AMANDA sits and continues to tell the audience her story. It is the first time she has told anybody.

I did go to a counsellor – once. I didn't say that "word," but I sort of told her what I did.

She lets out a big sigh.

I thought she would fix me up and I would walk out of there cured – but she didn't help. I went home and I binged worse than ever! So I never went back. I secretly went to my normal doctor too and told her. I thought she'd find some magical medical reason for why I had these cravings, but all she said was: "simply set your mind to it and quit. Just quit!" I wish I could! I mean, it makes sense – this is all so stupid there doesn't seem to be any reason why I shouldn't be able to. And I can!

AMANDA cheers up as she remembers that this is her last time.

Because that is exactly what this is!

She indicates the table full of food.

This is: "My Big Quit!" The Binge that is going to end all binges!

AMANDA pulls out a cooler.

I'd better make sure I use up everything.

She gets out a carton of ice cream.

Ice cream is great because I love it, and it slides up super easily.

She takes a spoonful, savouring it and thinking.

You know how I first learned how to do this? I was only in Grade Five and my teacher, Miss Anderson, was giving us our first health class in, you know, sex, and, well, I suddenly realized that I had never actually seen what a naked guy even looked like, so I went searching in the school library. I decided to try the medical section hoping a book would have a picture or something. Well, this huge yoga book caught my eye because it had this almost naked man on it's cover, wearing only this little diaper thing, doing all these contortions. I was looking through, hoping I could catch a glimpse, when I came to this chapter on cleansing. Here he was sitting cross-legged and he had a string going up one nostril and down the other and he was pulling it through to clean his nose! On the next page he had his stomach sucked in to about an inch wide and a little stream of water was pouring out of his mouth! It was called, "Cleansing the Stomach," and it said: "Blow out all your air, suck your stomach in, and let water pour out, or, if you must, give a small tickle at the back of the throat with your middle and index finger." Right away this idea popped into my head. I had just found out how fattening ice cream was, so that weekend I collected my allowance, hopped on my bicycle and raced down to the Dairy Queen. And I bought myself this huge, loaded banana split. I sat right down there on the curb and I gobbled it in, mouthful after delicious mouthful. Then, I got back on my bike and cycled home. Mom and Dad were working and my sister was out so I locked all the doors.

AMANDA physically remembers herself back into the story as she tells it. She remembers how sick she felt.

I slowly went to the bathroom, put the toilet seat up, blew out all my air and pumped in my stomach. Nothing happened. So I was about to put my fingers toward my mouth when there was this huge explosion! Warm milky water came blasting out of my mouth! And it didn't go into a nice little stream, it went everywhere! All over the floor, into the bathtub, up and over all the walls. And it kept coming, and it kept coming! And it went up and through my nose, and a piece of pineapple got stuck there, and there were bits of strawberries and blueberries and breakfast and – Yuk! I thought it was the grossest thing in all the world! I stopped. And I cleaned it all up, and I knew that I would never, *ever* do that again!

AMANDA stops for a moment, bringing herself back to the present.

And I never did. Not once! I didn't even think about it again...

AMANDA forces herself to face the truth.

...until I turned fifteen. Fifteen! I hated fifteen! I was great at fourteen. That's when this picture was taken.

AMANDA retrieves a beautiful picture of herself in a bathing suit. She has it somewhere special, perhaps hanging up, as an incentive for her diets.

But at fifteen I suddenly started to gain weight! I wasn't eating any more than usual but I was getting really fat. So I immediately started to diet. And at first I did great. I could easily lose five or six pounds in a week. But after awhile I started to gain the pounds back faster than I could lose them. And I began to have these cravings! I mean I'd really crrrraaave, for junky stuff like chocolate and cake! And the tension would grow and grow until I just broke down and ate. And then I'd hate myself!

So there I was, feeling fat and fifteen, and there was a big school dance coming up. I was on a really strict diet because I was trying to fit into this dress that I had borrowed from my sister, when suddenly, I lost it – and I ate a whole block of cheese melted in the microwave! I got so mad at myself and then "bang", I remembered! It was honestly the first time I had even thought about it since Grade Five! I went to the bathroom, and, well, it was still pretty gross but...

It seemed like magic. And during that year, every now and again, when I was in danger of gaining weight, I would simply go and throw up.

As AMANDA continues there is a sense that she is trying to figure all of this out for the first time.

But then, the next year, I started doing it not just once every couple of months, but more and more until I was throwing up almost every day! And now? Sometimes I can't stop for weeks! I eat for hours and then I throw up – and I think I'm okay and that I'll go back to my normal life – but then I end up eating for hours again so I have to throw up again.

I'm almost failing in school. I used to get A's and B's but now I am scraping by with C's. And I used to never get depressed but lately I can't make it out of bed sometimes and once, at school, the room went totally, literally, black.

I look at all my friends who I should be like, but I can't seem to get back to them... I wish I was with them now.

She stops and takes in where she actually is and looks at all the food on the table. This reminds her that she is working on quitting and she reaffirms her vow:

But I will be soon because this *is* my last time of *all* times and then I will be thin and perfect and happy again!

AMANDA takes out some leftover macaroni and eats one or two mouthfuls, mechanically. She is anything but happy as she faces the stark realities of her world.

Pasta is good for when you've eaten too much sweet stuff. There, that's better. Oh, and I can't forget this... (*presents the next food with a bitter singsong*) ...duddle dee du de dah...

She gets out a cake. There isn't any glee left. It's as though she despises the food.

A frozen Sara Lee chocolate cake! Oh, and my last time? I can't forget these... (*singsong*) ...duddle dee du de dah!

She gets out a full box of Turtle chocolates. She is very cynical.

A whole box of chocolates! I can sit around all afternoon like that Turtle Lady, (*sings*) "I love Turtles, yah yah yah!"

She clicks back to reality.

The caramel in them is really hard to get back up though.

She goes back to being cynical.

But, what helps that is another treat binge item, Coke!

A half-full, two litre bottle of Coke appears.

It sort of erodes everything before it comes up.

She takes a long drink. It seems to calm her a little. She looks out at the audience and goes on.

I must admit, my system is starting to break down. You know that little flap in the back of your throat that opens and closes when you eat? Well, I think mine is broken because the food just comes up automatically, even when I don't want it to... and quite often there's blood. And I've managed to wreck my teeth. The dentist told me I had eight thousand dollars worth of work to do on them. Eight thousand dollars! My parents just about died! He explained to them that it could be from an eating disorder called "Bulimia" because the acid in the stomach coming up erodes the teeth, or, he said, it could be hereditary. My parents immediately decided it was hereditary, but I know – and I'm sure the dentist knows, that it was from throwing up so much.

I did tell my parents about this thing. They do know! Right after I read that article I took it to them and I said:

AMANDA imagines herself talking to her parents:

"I do this."

She points to an imaginary magazine article.

"I don't know why. I know, it's *so* stupid. You don't have to worry! I am never going to do it again." They were glad I had talked to them, but then – we've never mentioned it since.

AMANDA wonders about this and then comes up with the answer.

I guess they really believed me when I said that I could quit!

AMANDA gets out a package of red licorice. It is the last thing she has hidden in her room.

For some strange reason if the last thing you eat is red licorice, it's also always the last thing that comes out, so you know when your stomach is empty. And I've started to throw up at half-hour intervals so nothing has the chance to turn into fat. Food, toilet, toilet, food, food, toilet, toilet...

AMANDA has indicated back and forth between the table and the toilet and finally lets her gaze rest upon the toilet. She surprises herself with her next realization.

I know a lot about toilets! I've done major research in different toilets! Can you imagine? I could give you all a lecture on the ideal toilet!

AMANDA goes further, becoming cynical again.

I could stand here, and call myself something like – Ms Upperchucker, here to talk to you all today about toilets.

AMANDA assumes the character of her imagined Ms Upperchucker.

"Rule Number One! Scout out a good toilet before starting a binge. You want to find a private one with a solid locking door. Nothing worse than being stuck in a cubicle throwing up and having to listen for other people coming in. But if that happens, then stop, turn your feet around and..."

She reverts back to being herself.

...pretend to blow your nose or something. I've waited in cubicles for hours while someone does their make-up or fixes their hair!

She goes back to being the lecturer but it is less pronounced.

"Rule Number Two! The best actual toilet is one without too much water in the bowl. That gives you a nice porcelain slide for the procedure.

AMANDA does a hand gesture of a slide.

A bowl full of water is terribly messy and noisy. But, again, if you're stuck, then flush the toilet, quickly throw-up a few times, then wait, and flush the toilet and throw up again. Or, sometimes there is a small dry space at the back and you can inch your head in there being careful not to touch the dirty lifted seat..."

AMANDA has stooped over to demonstrate but stops and goes back to herself as she digests the strangeness of it all. She continues quietly and seriously.

My father took so much time teaching us children about proper hygiene for public washrooms. Sometimes, I wonder what he would think if he ever saw my face scrunched up to a toilet seat and covered in puke.

She gathers herself to press on.

I mean, I know every toilet in my high school – all the ones at my friend's houses – the best ones downtown. I even know lots of toilets around this province – Heck! I know toilets across Canada!

AMANDA takes a long drink of Coke.

And I can see each one of them. Because once you've been head to head with them, you really know them well.

AMANDA gulps down more Coke. She settles in to tell a final story. As she recounts the story she puts herself more and more into it so by the end it is as though she is there.

Like this one toilet in Toronto. I'll never forget that toilet. I was there with my parents but they had dropped me off at a movie by myself. Halfway through this weird thing happened. I began to see all these amazing pastries that we had passed on the way to the theatre. So I got up – left – and found myself back at the bakery. The next thing I knew I was sitting on this park bench, surrounded by all these gooey cakes that I was gobbling up. And suddenly I felt really really full. Only I had forgotten to do that number one rule. Find a good bathroom first. So I began searching, feeling sicker and sicker – and I couldn't find one anywhere. Finally – I was directed to this one down a long, dark, dead-end alley. I knew I was not in the safest part of Toronto, but I also knew I had to go down there. So I did.

AMANDA physically goes down the imaginary alley and into the bathroom.

And at the end was this tiny bathroom – and you go in – and – it was so filthy. You could smell the urine – the sink was covered in guck – there was brown smeared all over the toilet, no toilet paper – nothing. But I knew I had to do it, only, I had also forgotten to drink anything.... So I had to get some water out of that sink–

She sees the sink vividly.

–and I did. I drank some water – and I threw up. And I drank more water, and I threw up. And I did it again and again until I was completely empty – finished. "A New Beginning." And I was never going to do that again! So, I got out of there–

She leaves the area of her imagined bathroom.

–and I was walking back down the alley when this man started coming towards me, staring at me. I tried to pass him but he grabbed me and rammed himself against me. I hit—and I managed to get away—but I didn't have anywhere to go except back in here.

AMANDA has gone back into her imagined bathroom.

So I locked the door and he banged and yelled all this crude stuff.... Then everything went quiet, and I waited – trapped in this horrible, stinking bathroom that I had just thrown up in. And then there was this rustling outside – and under the door came these grossest, most violent, obscene pictures – using all these little kids.... And they kept coming, and they kept coming, and all I could think of was that this was all my fault! My fault. I had put myself here, in this bathroom, to throw up. And I vowed right then that I would never, ever do this again – throw up again.

AMANDA stops and lets herself slowly come back to the present. She takes a look at the toilet, her bedroom, and all the food laid out and faces the stark reality that if the Toronto episode had not made her quit, this probably wouldn't be her last time either.

That was two years ago. I've thrown up hundreds of times since then.

She goes over to the food on the table and questions herself.

My last time? "My Last Ever In My Whole Life Binge"? Somehow – I don't think so...

She looks out at the audience.

I think I need help.

She takes up her journal.

Ha. My success journal. Usually, I would rip these pages out and start again. But this time, this time, I'm going to keep them, with their chocolate sauce and icing sugar. This may not be my last binge, but it is the first one I'm going to walk away from without throwing up. White rabbits, white rabbits, white rabbits. A new chapter, "Finding Help." There must be some councillor out there who can help me.

AMANDA takes one last look at all the uneaten food, then slowly, with strength, she turns and exits.

The end.

Afterword
— — • — • — —

I would like to say a few words about my own recovery from bulimia. I had always thought it would be a momentous occasion to be celebrated year after year: "The Day I Beat the Big B!" But it didn't work out that way. It was many years ago that I, like Amanda at the end of the play, knew I had a serious problem and set forth to solve it, but when did I actually stop being bulimic? There is no exact date. At first I'd go three days without throwing up, then a week, then a month, then two months! Then, just as I thought my struggles were behind me, I'd slip up again. The path to success was a gradual process that lasted about six years.

I had also thought that I would find one magic cure or answer to my problem. In the search for this answer I read many books on self awareness, on diets, and on health and eating disorders. My reading made me realize that instead of having just the problem of throwing up, I had many blocked areas to examine and release. From the books, I learned valuable exercises for self-esteem which I did religiously in the hope of emerging from my dark tunnel and, gradually, I began to see glimmers of light through the process. Each book was a step that brought me closer to freedom.

Along with my books I went to several counsellors, but I never lasted more than a few visits. Looking back, I realize that it would have helped to keep looking for a professional counsellor with whom I felt truly comfortable. My parents did try to help me through my roughest periods but I was never truly honest with them so their generosity was impaired.

One of the strongest driving forces behind my recovery was the support of a close friend. I checked in with her regularly and honestly through many years, sharing my triumphs, my defeats, my slip ups and my discoveries. We spent a fortune on champagne which we would "pop off" to cheer me onwards after my discouraging set backs. It was this constant "checking-in" that kept me in touch with reality and helped me to continue towards a healthier lifestyle.

Am I completely recovered? A few years ago I didn't think complete recovery was possible. Though I no longer threw up, I thought I'd always be afraid of food, afraid of getting fat, afraid of "The Big Binge." I was constantly on a diet and constantly weighing myself. I fasted for days if I was acting in a play and my costumes were revealing ones, and I dreaded the fittings, afraid I may have gained weight since my measurements were taken. I would look at the beautiful women in the dressing room and wish for their slim waists, their thin legs, or their sleek arms. It was not until recently, when I was writing my play and again reading books on eating disorders, that I began to see the diet trap that one could get entangled in, and realized that I was snared.

I had never before thought about the long-term implications of dieting, presuming a particular diet was over and done with once the pounds were shed. One theory that fascinated me was that our metabolism still worked as it did thousands of years ago when our food supply was directly dependent upon a successful hunt or upon our crops. After a time of famine, our body would immediately try to get fat to prepare for any future crisis. Suddenly my never-ending, yo-yo weight pattern made sense. I had always thought that someone was fat because they ate huge desserts and didn't do any exercise when, in reality, they may have dieted the pounds on!

I began to wonder about my obsession to look "slim." Who defined what I "should" look like? Was it me? Or was it our society and an enormous industry of fashion, diet, and make-up? I remembered a passionate paragraph I had written when I was eight, railing against people who judged someone by their looks and not by who they were inside. I wondered when I had first judged myself by my exterior and when I began to judge others by theirs.

In the midst of "weighing" all these questions, I delivered a beautiful, healthy baby boy. And, surprise of all surprises, I did not immediately lose the extra 50 pounds that I had gained! When I went to get dressed I took one look at my tiny pair of pre-pregnancy jeans and I knew I was in trouble. I waited for the panic to set in. Dieting was out of the question since I did not want to jeopardize the baby's health. What could I do? I decided that for the first time in my adult life, I would not worry about my poundage: I would let my body weight adjust itself naturally. I was amazed at how relieved I was by this decision, and surprised that my days were just as alive and fun as when I was slim. My weight took about eight months to adjust itself to twenty pounds more than I'd ever before allowed myself to weigh. Again, I was astonished to discover that I did not mind. I felt healthy and even beautiful! I began to look at people around me and instead of criticizing their body shape, marvel at how unique and extraordinary they were.

Am I completely recovered today? I can honestly say yes. My weight no longer dictates to me who I am and how I should feel. I am free. It is the first true freedom I have experienced since childhood.

A Prop Note
— — • — — • — —

There is a certain prop in the play that is meaningful to me as a performer, but that the audience does not get to experience. It is Amanda's diary and the pages she rips out. With the fear that it may be indulgent to reveal such raw material, I'd like to include some selected, unedited entries from my own personal journals. I don't have any from my very sick days. Like Amanda, I threw them all out, but I did find some scattered entries I kept during the years I was trying to recover.

Diary of a Bulimic

MAY 31ˢᵀ, 1980
Strange – me? How did this all happen – why? I understand more about the losing of a precious hour, day, week, month. The month of May. In my worst hours, when my poor tummy is stuffed and my head is sore and reeling, I am still in the background. A small tiny voice in the back of my neck, waiting to be set free.

I hope the time has come. I feel I have experienced and learned more than I ever would have, had I stayed sane, but I think the time has come to file the experience and get on with my life – so maybe this time it will happen.

So I close another month. I believe one can do anything that they really want. I can too. I've succumbed enough to know that I want to be set free. So, I swear, as of this hour, I shall try.

JUNE 1ˢᵀ, 1980
Who – me? What? Made it through one super day? Holy Smokes! I am afraid of the overpowering need for a binge that may come over me still tonight. I've never been in jail. I've always been free to take the dive down. But the feeling when I am on a binge of having to know where the next junk food is going to come from while still swallowing my tenth chocolate bar – makes me think that an addict in jail must go through hell. But I made it through today.

JUNE 2ⁿᵈ, MIDNIGHT, 1980
I'm disgusted, fed up, ready to throw my life away. But then that is what I've been doing for the past months anyway. Only Day Two and I'm crying again.

JUNE 10ᵀᴴ, 1980
I'm no farther ahead. It seems I've listed my priorities so many times – only to forget them at the crucial moment. From this moment I can only try once more and say good riddance to chocolate, sugar, and chemicals and hello to me. I swear by my true self, me, that I will.

JUNE 14TH, 1980

I remember my loneliness of Valentine's Day. There was a gentle breeze and though I had plugged my body, the breeze breathed a fresh hope. This evening, once again, I feel that breeze and write through my experience upon the subject of my habit in the hope of figuring it out.

The cycle begins with withdrawal. The mind and body feel sick and cry out forcefully for relief. Motives are warped. Freedom means a place to black out the world and binge.

Stage two is eating. I tell myself that a mouthful is all I need, but deep inside I know that once I've begun, I won't be able to stop.

The final stage is the most pleasant one, providing the stomach is not too stretched so pain masks the mind's relief. It is from this final stage that I now write. I make plans for tomorrow. Since I have put myself near the bottom of my despair hole I have something to strive for, a place to climb to. I can plan: "Tomorrow I will fast."

Meanwhile, deep inside, I know I shall have to contend with the beginning of the cycle again tomorrow. I have been at this long enough to know I am in trouble. I have said, "this is the last time" enough to know the chances of it really being the last time are slim. For three weeks I've been trapped and I can feel myself being wheeled toward destruction where I won't be able to return. Many times in stage two I've thought of how useless and undesirable is the life I am leading. I know it is dangerous. If only the tears of regret that come near the end of stage two could be moved to stage one. I am better not eating at all. Actually feel quite good after a few days like that, but I cannot abstain forever from food like alcohol or drugs. How can I think so clearly and yet be so screwed up!

NOVEMBER 3RD, 1981

I am determined to become a healthy soul and body before this diary turns into another year! I shall listen to my body from inside, as I have been learning to do, and unravel the bottom of this iceberg. I will write whenever I want to get out the thoughts and feelings that may otherwise lead to the habit of hell.

1:35 p.m. My head is sore. The mind thinks of ways to make me feel better, like sugar food. Mucky is my head. I think I'll walk. I feel at a loss for things to do but I know there are things out there.

10:35 p.m. I get my sticker for an accomplished non-heave-up day!

NOVEMBER 4TH, 1981

Whew, it seems ages since I started this diary, yesterday. My head is full, but not grumpy, just not too bright. My body is all plugged up. I know I ate too much last night, by the scale I gained three pounds. I am afraid of getting fat, but what is that compared to the hell life of the habit? I did everything on my list and I feel good. Boy, I build, create and carry a lot of tension!

NOVEMBER 5ᵀᴴ, 1981

Now I woke up feeling quite bright this morning and proud of myself for having such a wonderful day before!

12:07 I am at this moment on the verge of an upset. I thought I'd go swimming at 11:30. I decided I didn't want to. My head began to feel at loose ends. I ate a banana, then still feeling frustration went on eating rice and salad. A small voice saying, "Watch out, you won't be able to stop." Another voice yelling, "Go for it and get rid of it!" I will lie down and get up and have my proper lunch I planned. Seems easy. All so sensible. But it is so hard!

NOVEMBER 6ᵀᴴ, 1981

I am proud, proud, proud of myself!

NOVEMBER 16ᵀᴴ, 1981

My weight is doing strange and wonderful things! I'm used to it bouncing way up unless I keep control of it through Bulimia – but this week it has kept pretty steady! Even when I woke up like this morning and thought – "Oh no! I'm going to have to starve for a while, the scales are going to register a ton" – they don't, making me quite gleeful.

NOVEMBER 17ᵀᴴ, 1981

I love this "Diary of a Bulimic." I must say it helps me so much.

DECEMBER 1ˢᵀ, 1981

I don't believe it! I am on the verge of throwing up!! I've already eaten more than is good for me and just hummed through the fridge wondering what I could gobble!

DECEMBER 2ᴺᴰ, 1981

Whew! Yesterday I came closer to binging than I have for a long long time!

DECEMBER 7ᵀᴴ, 1981

Ahhhhhhhhhhhhhhhhh! I did it AGAIN!!!!!
The pressure built,
My unhealth grew,
the day went on,
but my clear thought flew – away.

I tried to grasp,
I tried to hold,
But something snapped,
and I started to fold,
I ate one, two, four things,
And then took the dive:
Into the gray land,
where I cease to exist,
My self deeply covered,
In piles of mist.

Hours cruise by,
each more painful than the last,
until I purge to deep bottom
And sink to the past.
And here slowly stroke upward,
And gasp in new air,
And strike out again,
to myself try to be fair.
Which brings me to now,
as tired, depleted, I write,
I hang to hope—from now on
My struggles will direct me alright.
Whewwwwwwwww.

JANUARY 20TH, 1982

It seems like a year since I last was on the surface of life, cruising along in my sail boat.

On December 7th, 1981 my boat rocked over and I took on some water. I bailed that out but then for the rest of the month I had around ten more spills. It seemed I'd almost get my ship sailing on path again but I'd oversee or neglect some maintenance work and over I'd go! I did manage to steer my ship safely into Christmas Week and had a wonderful and successful time then.

However, the first two weeks in January brought a major upset. My ship went over on January 4th and I have been floundering in the stormy seas since! I did have various days that I surfaced to keep my breath and life but I never got the bailing done. This brings me to today. It is pouring with rain outside. Had a lovely silent walk. I have a glimpse, for the first time ever, of my potential as a human being and life force. This glimpse gives me a reason to strive forward and grab onto that potential and sail with it. Like harnessing the winds. Like focus. Today I will begin again sorting out, clearing out, and tidying up my ship.

JANUARY 28TH, 1982

I have a sense inside of me,
Of what that me can possibly be.
Out there in the world where everything's busy,
I now can survive without getting dizzy.
I can keep my joy of life all safe,
My security and visions live through the fast pace.
To love one's self is to love the world,
And to love the world—in all its turmoil,
Is Freedom.

FEBRUARY 4TH, 1982

I feel tired and like a slug. Yesterday I overfed. Some is still with me today. "Heellpp!" It is my birthday tomorrow. It was my "be beautiful" deadline. I see now that is warped. I am a beauty now, yesterday and today. I try to remember the wonderful feelings when I was young. It is natural I make eating mistakes. I am discovering and learning. I am making my way out of the labyrinth I constructed in my mind these past twenty years, clearing paths behind me to go ahead. Today I shall breathe deeply. Thanks Diary.

FEBRUARY 7TH, 1982

Feeling wonderful. (My head keeps saying I am fat. I'll just yell back three times "wonderful, wonderful, wonderful!") Now where was I – ah yes, on my way out the door...

FEBRUARY 8TH, 1982

I thought, as I ate another frozen cookie: "I'd rather be doing something else." In the old days I was wanting to avoid the "something else's," or I was in such a pit of despair I wanted to escape. Not yesterday. Yes, I blew it, but I think I am going onward – somehow – still.

JULY 1ST, 1982

A new part of my book. A new chapter, so to speak. I always expected the world and my life to be rosy, wonderful and perfect, especially once I quit my bad habit, but that world is impossible. I quit my habit but my life was not great, pressure built, worry mounted, and life sometimes seemed no easier than when I binged. My perception of the wonderful world has to change. Yes, it does. If I fall, I can cry and still have fulfilling moments, but if I criticize or blame regarding the fall or worry about the next – "POW" there goes the easy flow. Here comes the binge. I am changing, slowly but surely.

NOVEMBER 7TH, 1982

Well – it has been five months!! I can hardly believe it!

NOVEMBER 12TH, 1982

Whoopee! Another star day on my calendar!

NOVEMBER 17TH, 1982

A star day! It was a toughie though. Lot's of "you're fat," "worthless," "can't stand this," "can't stand that," thoughts going round my head.

DECEMBER 17TH, 1982

It is so hard writing my "Success Journal" after a setback! It has taken me until eight-thirty the following night to begin. But I must remember that the day had success even through the upset.

DECEMBER 31ST, 1982

New Year's Resolutions are popping into my mind. This is a huge step. For years I've not been able to make any as the one big problem was impossible to conquer.

Now I see it disappearing behind me.

MARCH 11TH, 1983

I did wonderfully – until February this year! I made my first slip up then – sllllide to old habit! Like a first cigarette it turned into ten. Ten times. Or less. But there. I have to catch hold of some ground. Breathe. Release. Let go to travel onward.

APRIL 12TH, 1983

I just wrote a cold turkey vow. I can't believe how fast I can slide into a nightmare world of depression, despair, avoidance, denial of me, just like the olden days.

I know I must trust the new me deep inside who is beginning to emerge, know I have not killed it but just need to open some windows and let the sun in again.

JUNE 19TH, 1983

Too many slip ups!!! And I hate, yes, hate what they do to me – my tongue, my teeth, my head. I struggle onward.

JANUARY, 1984

My little diary. You are full of me. My pains, my mix-ups, my me-ness. When storms come up I must remember that it is my perception of the adventures of these storms that will sail me through them. Champagne on a rainy afternoon day off, by myself, to celebrate my six months of clean living behind me and to toast the adventures ahead. *Bon Courage, Bon Chance.*

Je me souviens

memories of an expatriate anglophone,
montrealaise, quebecoise, exiled in Canada

Lorena Gale

Born in Montreal, **Lorena Gale** is an award-winning actress, director and writer who has worked extensively in theatres across Canada. Her first play *Angelique* was the winner of the duMaurier National Playwriting Competition and was nominated Outstanding New Play in Calgary's Betty Mitchell Awards 98. Her solo performance, *Je me souviens: memories of an expatriate anglophone, Montrealaise, Quebecoise exiled in Canada*, premiered in Eastern Front Theatre's On the Waterfront Festival in Halifax and was produced at One Yellow Rabbit's High Performance Rodeo in Calgary, The Firehall Theatre in Vancouver and the Belfry Theatre in Victoria. Lorena lives in Vancouver with her husband and son.

Je me souviens was first produced by the Firehall Arts Centre, in co-production with Curious Tongue and Touchstone Theatre Company, Vancouver, British Columbia in January, 2000, with the following company:

LORENA   Lorena Gale

Directed by John Cooper
Lighting design by Gerald King
Slide Design by Tim Matheson
Sound Design by John McCulloch
Choreography by Denise Lonewalker and Lorena Gale
Stage Managed by Diana Stewart Imbert

— — • — — • — —

It was subsequently produced by Belfry Theatre Company, in co-production with Curious Tongue in February, 2000, with the same company.

— — • — — • — —

Je me souviens was presented as a work-in-progress at On the Waterfront Festival by Eastern Front Theatre Company in Dartmouth, Nova Scotia in May 1998, and at One Yellow Rabbit's High Performance Rodeo, Calgary, Alberta in January 1999.

First published in 2001 by Talonbooks. Reprinted with permission.

Characters

LORENA

Je me souviens
memories of an expatriate anglophone,
montrealaise, quebecoise, exiled in Canada
— — • — — • — —

Black. Music. Robert Charlebois' "Lindberg" bleeds into "This Land is your Land, This Land is my Land." The sound of a needle being scraped over a record as it is taken off. Lights up. Slide of Joe's Café. Ambient "café" sound.

LORENA

I am on Commercial Drive, sitting in Joe's Café. I'd just bumped into another expatriate and like those from "the old country," hungry for news from home, whenever we meet we all always reminisce or share news of the others we have left behind. It is a ritual of love and remembrance played out on alien soil by *emigrés* all over the world. Only we're in Vancouver and home is Montreal. The same country. At least, today it is.

We speak in English, my first language and her second. We speak in English because I don't know Greek. We speak candidly, without forethought, without apology. Around us we hear snatches of Italian, Arabic, Spanish, Portuguese, Cantonese, Urdu, etc. We speak unashamedly and to each other.

So I say to my compatriot, "I have just come back from Montreal. I can't believe how much it's changed. Everything for sale. Everything for rent. Liquidation. Going out of Business. And everywhere these tacky dollar stores. And they're the only ones who seem to be doing any real business. It's sad. I have never seen Montreal looking so bad."

And the next thing I know, there's this long haired, grunged out, French guy in my face saying, "Hey! You don't say that! You don't talk about Montréal!"

He had been listening in on our private conversation, which had obviously offended him, and had half risen from his seat to stretch across his table and point an accusatory finger at me, like he was the long arm of the Language Police and had nabbed himself another Anglo traitor. His look was irate and triumphant like one spoiling for a fight. My friend immediately put her head down like somebody trying to avoid one. Me...? I was stunned into momentary silence.

What could I have possibly said to offend him? That Montreal looked poorly and depressed? The truth? For a second there, I thought I was in a Café on St. Denis St. a little too drunk, voicing my insensitive Anglo opinions on the political situation a little too loud, and this brave soldier in the struggle for Quebec independence was standing forth to eradicate this heretic from their midst.

I looked around expecting to see a room full of hostile and contemptuous people... but no one was paying attention. I was still in Lotus Land. And what did I care since I wasn't talking to him anyway. So I told him to "fuck off and mind his own business."

"No! You fuck off! It is my business. Me, I'm from Montréal. I know. You. You don't say nothing. *Tu n'a pas le droit!*"

I don't have the right? I don't have the right!?

My friend hates confrontation. She tells me to "...ignore him. He's an asshole. He's just looking for a fight. Come on. Let's go somewhere else."

But I have gone somewhere else. Thirty six hundred miles to somewhere else! And I cannot back down.

"I don't have the right! Why? Because I'm English? Why? Because I'm Black?!"

"Ah, you. You don't know nothing."

"Oh! *Je sais, moé. Je sais assez que toi, èsti. Et si je n'avais rien su, j'aurais eu le meme droit de parler que toi!*"

"*Toi? Tu parle Français?!*"

"*Oui. Je parle Français. Je vien de Montréal, moé. Je suis Montréalaise. Je suis nee a Montréal. Et j'ai le droit a parler. Le meme droit a parler que toi, oèsti! Avec n'importe qui, n'importe ou.* Okay? So fuck off!".

"Eh, eh, eh! *C'est correct. Je m'èxcuse.* You come from Montréal. I thought.... You know, I from Montreal too, eh. And I thought..."

He picked up his backpack and wandered out on to The Drive. My friend was examining the residue at the bottom of her cappuccino. She hadn't said a word though the entire altercation and I could tell she wanted to go too. I still wanted to share my memories of Montreal. But the moment was lost. She had to run. And so we parted.

    Slide – exterior of Joe's Cafe.

You know, I'd see him on the Drive, from time to time, with a group of other young Quebecois beneath the rainbow outside of Joe's Cafe. His shoulders hunched from the weight of his pack. His long hair matting into incongruous dreds. He is all passion and gesture and speaks French with a fury so familiar but I can no longer follow. And when I pass, he mumbles "*Salute,*" in grudging recognition.

We are both, after all, from the same place. His Montréal is my Montreal. His Québec is the Quebec of my birth. Like heads and tails, we are two faces of the same coin. One side inscribed in French. The other English. And we are both so far from home.

I am an expatriate anglophone, Montrealaise, Quebecoise exiled in Canada. And I remember. *Je me souviens...*

> *White out. Gille Vigneault's "Mon Pays." Dreamlike sound. The soft whistling of wind.*

Je me souviens d'un reve que j'avais souvent depuis mon enfance. Dans ce rève c'est l'hiver. Et je suis toute seule dans une plaine. Une grande plaine de neige. Y'a de la neige partout. Autant que les yeux peuvent voir. Pas d'arbres. Pas de maisons. Rien que de la neige. De la neige qui n'a pas été defiguré. Immacule. Implacable. Pur.

Le soleil est un cercle parfait d'un jaune foncé, suspendu dans un ciel qui est bleu, bleu et clair. Et c'est froid. Tellement froid. Si froid... que ca pique. Et la lumiere du soleil sur la neige... aveuglante! Je veux rentrer chez moi, mais je ne sais pas ou je suis. Aucune signe de civilisation. Je suis perdue. Je suis perdue dans une plaine de neige aveuglante.

> *Light change.*

(*as Ethel, a West Indian woman*) You know what de problem is wit you Canajun Blacks? You don't know where you come from. Ya don know who y'are. Ya talk like Whitey. Ya act all so-so like Whitey. Hell. You even move like you gotta a rod shoved up to your arse to brain. All jig-jig like a puppet. And dat's de problem wit' you. You let the White man into your head and now you all messed up. You don tink straight. You Black on de outside, White on the inside. You're assimilated. Assimilated Negroes. Dat's what you are."

> *Slide – "When people ask me which island I come from, I say Montreal. And they look confused. When people tell me to go back where I came from - I look confused."*

> *SFX – Opening notes to theme from Star Trek. Slides – Little Burgundy.*

(*as Captain Kirk*) Star date nineteen hundred and sixty one.

We have have been living among a small tribe of coloured outcasts in an area of the city known today as Little Burgundy – located within the outer perimeter of the downtown central core. Our crew, assembled from Jamaica, Sri Lanka, New Guinea, Bermuda and St. Catherine's, Ontario, have spent more than 75 earth years and three human generations in this location. But our work here has come to an end.

May 1st 0800 hrs. We leave Downtown. Travelling at warp speed east along Dorchester, north on Park Avenue, west on Bernard and north again on

Durocher. Successfully circumventing Mont Royal – the pimple local inhabitants call a mountain, in the middle of the city.

We have set a course for Outremont. Our mission – to seek life in new neighbourhoods. To boldly go where no black has gone before! *(sings "Star Trek" theme)*

> *Light change.*

> *Soundscape: English, French, Dutch, German, Italian, Hebrew, Yiddish, Arabic, Russian. In hushed whispers.*

(as LORENA) French filters through as ambient sound and English is spoken heavily and accented. Our new neighbours names are Van Doorn, Petrovich, Leiberman, Mancini, Papanicalopolis, Osler, Azra. Each one speaks a language I cannot understand and sounds stranger to me than I am sure I look to them.

Men with payos and long dark coats and fur rimmed hats, even in summer, huddle in the middle of the sidewalk passionately discussing the Torah in Yiddish. Greek mothers hang out their windows and holler for their kids, "Yanni. Stavros. *Ella tho."* Italian men in cotton undershirts sit on kitchen chairs drinking wine out on the stoop and smack their kids for stealing a sip.
Did we really move across the city or to another continent?

"Immigrants", my mother calls them. " Beings from another country. Not born here like us."

But no one is like us in Outremont.

They say...

> *SFX – (In different languages) "Go back where you came from."*

But I cannot understand them.

> *Light change.*

Mr. Camille lives next door. He is a friendly old man with watery eyes and splotchy red skin and sits on his balcony chain smoking Players Plain and rocking back and forth. Sometimes he sends me to Finasts to get his cigarettes. But I am not allowed to cross the street, so I go up to Franks, which is on the same side. And when I get back he gives me a nickel! He tried to give me a dime once but I gave it back. Nickels were better. They're bigger than dimes.

Mrs. Camille only wears cotton house dresses with faded floral patterns and the same tanned cardigan. Whenever you see her she has a smile on her face, but I know... she cries all the time. I know because my bedroom wall is shared with theirs. I often hear her muffled sobbing, moaning, sometimes wailing on the other side. She tries to hide it, but I can tell. Her eyes are as red as the smile she paints on her face.

(as a child) "Mr. Camille? Why does Mrs. Camille cry all the time...?

(as Mr. Camille) My vife. She is not alvays so happy. But vhy should you care? You are just a little girl? Vhy vould a little girl vant to know such things? Vhat can I tell you that you vould understand? *(Sits)* Vhy does Mrs. Camille cry? How can I explain?

Do you know vhat is Holocaust? No. You are too young to know this. Do you know what are Jews? Mrs. Camille and I, ve are Jews. Jewish people. And ve are... different! Yes. Vherever ve go in the world ve are different. Maybe not so much here. But ve are different.

Some people in the vorld... they don't like different. Some people in the vorld think they are so much better than everyone else. Not because they do things that are extraordinary or good. No. They just *think* they are better. And they vant every one to be like them. This, of course, is impossible. But this is vhat they vant. And if you are not like them, if you are different.... Then they persecute you. Try to control you. Enslave you. To kill you.

Ve Jews for many centuries vere slaves. Yes, just like you and your African people. Ve too vere slaves once. But slavery is not tolerated so vell anymore. So they persecuted us. Tried to kill us. All of us. And this is what is the Holocaust. But some of us escape. *(lifts up his shirt sleeve and shows his wrist.)* See? Vhenever you see this you will know it was a Jew who escaped death.

Mrs. Camille... she escaped too. But many, many millions did not escape. Mrs. Camille's mother, Mrs. Camille's father, her sister Yeti, her brother David. All vere lost in the holocaust. And that is vhy Mrs. Camille cries sometimes. She cries because she misses her family.

You are a smart girl, I think. Smart enough to ask qvestions. Yes? The answers maybe you don't like or understand so vell. But one day everything will make sense to you. I vant you to remember vhat I'm telling you. Because you too are different. And it is important that you remember.

These people, who think they are so great—they are so superior—these people are everyvhere! Yes. These bad people are still all around us. Even here. In this Montreal. Today. That is vhy you and me... ve must never forget who ve are. Because ve are different, ve must remember. Because if ve forget, it could happen all over again. Do you understand? *(pause)* Good.

Now take your nickel and go buy some candy. I have had enough of your qvestions for one day. And don't ask Mrs. Camille. She doesn't like to talk about it. Go!

Light change. Music – "Shaboom Shaboom."

(*as LORENA*) Outremont, Montreal, Quebec. The Sixties. Before Star Trek. Before "Black Power." Before "Say it loud, I'm Black and I'm proud." Before "Black is beautiful." Black people were said to have hair like steel wool, liver lips and some people even believed we had tails.

"Don't ever let a white man rub your head!" my mother warned. Like the fat polished tummy of a Buddha, they would rub your head for luck.

My mother cleans like one possessed and dresses me for Sunday every day. The whole flat sparkles with a maniacal gleam and I too am squeaky clean and proper. When she's not cleaning, she's working – cutting loose threads and sewing labels on children's clothes delivered in large boxes to the flat. Or studying into the wee hours for her nursing exams.

She says they think we are dirty and lazy. So we must always be careful how we present ourselves. We must always put our best foot forward and strive to excel excellence. Hard work and cleanliness are the key.

I don't know who "they" are. I don't care what "they" think. I want to play. Instead I sit like Atlas on the balcony and watch the other grubby children on the ground below rev imaginary engines in their Dinky cars, making roads in the dust.

(*as Lillian*) Don't be asking me to go down there. There is nothing on these streets for you. And I won't have you running around like some wild street urchin trying to find that out. Don't you know that's what they expect from us? You've got everything you need right here. So make yourself content.

Beat.

I know you think you think I'm being hard on you right now. But you have got to understand. We're coloured and we're living in the white man's world. Don't think for a moment that you can do like they do.

Slide - "How to get by in the white man's world."

Jazzoid music. Upstage with pointer. Slide – a list which LORENA reads:

Don't talk back.
Don't raise your voice.
Don't wear loud colours.
Don't do anything to draw attention to yourself.
Smile even when it hurts.
Just try to fit in.
And don't rock the boat.

If any one stops to speak to you, answer them politely and only if you have to.
Otherwise keep on moving.
Walk like you know where you're going.
Keep focused on what's ahead of you.
If you run into some commotion, don't stand around gawking.
Don't try to help.
Just keep on moving.
If it looks like trouble is coming towards you then cross the street.
If it looks like trouble is sneaking up behind you then run.
If you're surrounded, then fight.
Keep your eyes and ears open at all times.
But if you find yourself in a situation – don't go to a policeman and don't stand still.
Just keep on moving and you'll be safe.

Slide – "He who fights and runs away, lives to fight another day.

SFX – The nigger chorus. Nigger repeated in many different languages.

Outremont Montreal Quebec Canada. We are called "nigger" in two official languages, as well as several unofficial others. "Black," too, is fighting word. But sounds like "Negro" in so many languages, I do not respond. My brother's fists fly daily.

But! ...It is the English slur that is the slur of choice. Even with French kids, who find that "negress noire" does not have the same rhythmic impact. Anglo, franco and allophone children walk in packs behind you, chanting: "niggerblack, niggerblack, niggerblack," on the way to school. All the way to school. I walk alone.

Light change.

SFX – loud bell. Slide – The Union Jack.

(*as a child*) I pledge allegiance to this flag and the Commonwealth for which it stands.

(*sings*) God shave our gracious Queen. Shave her with shaving cream. God shave the queen. Send her to Halifax. Make her pay all the tax...

Miss Bennett, an English grade school teacher, cuts through...

(*as Miss Bennet*) Enough! Good morning class.

(*wiggles like a bored child*) Good morning Miss Bennett.

(as Miss Bennett) Open your geography books to page 37, chapter six. "Bunga of the Jungle."

Snaps. Lights go out. Slide – "Bunga of the Jungle."

The jungle is a rain forest located in the Belgian Congo. The heart of deepest, darkest Africa. Can anybody tell us about Africa? Lorena?

Silence.

Bunga is an African. Africans are little primitive peoples with black skin – Lorena. And tight woolly hair – Lorena. And broad flat noses, who run about the jungle naked, climbing trees for fruit, digging in the earth with crudely shaped tools for tubers and nuts, and killing elephants with poison darts they blow through long tubes. Well... *(chuckles and pats LORENA's chair)* Maybe not you.

Oh! While we're on the subject... *(snaps and the lights come up)* There are many starving children in Africa. As you can imagine, they don't have lots of good things to eat like we have here. They don't have milk to drink, or mashed potatoes, or grilled cheese sandwiches on Wonderbread. They sleep right on the floor in houses made of straw—that don't even have any walls—and drink out of the same watering holes with the zebras and crocodiles. Well. These poor children obviously need our help.

Takes out an orange Unicef box.

That's why every year the good people at UNICEF ask nice Canadian children, like yourselves, to take this little box with them on Halloween and collect donations along with their trick or treats. The money you raise will be used to buy food, water, building materials and even a few school books for all the poor hungry people in Africa. So, don't forget to pick up your UNICEF box before you leave the school. In fact, I'll just leave one right here on Lorena's desk. A helpful reminder.

Now, where was I...

Lights change. SFX – music, party ambience.

(as LORENA) There are voices in the night. Dark voices. Warm as gingerbread and comfortingly familiar. It's Saturday night and the folks have come up from downtown. My uncles, my sister's school friends. And they've brought chicken from the Chalet Lucerne! I can smell it sweet and pungent through the stench of cigarette smoke. And in the morning there will be a wing, my favourite part, saved for me.

The Young Rascals croon softly in the background "Grooving on a Sunday afternoon..."

A male voice rises. A murmured female reply. Then the multi-pleasured laughter of a mellowed crowds response. Something groooovy is going on and I want to be a part of it.

> *SFX – "A coloured man walks into a greasy spoon and sits at the lunch counter. Then the waitress come over and says 'Sorry we don't serve niggers here.' The coloured man says 'That's alright. I don't eat them.'*

Laughter explodes like a raisin in the sun, rising beyond humour to an almost hysterical crescendo. Then diminishes into painful recognition. Followed by silence. Interminable and dense. And when they speak again, their tones are hushed and somber.

> *As what a child hears. Listening through the crack of light of a door ajar.*

There's a man with a dream.... And a woman on the bus.... And a young boy hanging from a tree.... The Panthers have left the jungle and have moved to the city... cause there's a war overseas... and coloured people are supposed to be free! They say the days of slavery are over... but the men in white hoods snatch you at night! That's why Chicago's burning...! People are sitting in Arkansas! People are sitting in Alabama! Malcolm. No, Martin. No, Martin. No, Malcolm. No, Martin is going to overcome.

> *Slide – "Change." SFX – "When are we all going to be free?"*

> *Slide – "Change." SFX – "I remember when they wouldn't serve us in the restaurants on St. Catherine's St. Or let us in the movie theatres..."*

> *Slide – "Change." SFX – "We have our rights."*

> *Slide – "Change." SFX – "Education is the key."*

> *Slide – "Change." SFX – "By any means necessary."*

> *Slide – "Change." SFX – "Yet lift me up!"*

> *SFX different voices –*
> *"Hey. We could be doing a lot worse. We could be living in The States. Or South Africa with that apartheid shit. I'd say we're damned lucky to be Canadians."*
> *"When was the last time you tried to get out of downtown?"*
> *"Oh, that doesn't mean anything. We have the laws to protect us."*
> *"Yeah. At least we don't have to worry about crosses burning and getting lynched."*
> *"Amen"*
> *"But folks are dying in America. For our rights."*

The debate rages into the night. I fall asleep with my ear to the door.

(Light change) SFX – Bagpipes. Feedback. Announcer on a P.A.

(as announcer) Guy Drummond Elementary School proudly presents...
Multicultural Day!

From Scotland...

Does the Highland Fling. Smiles and bows.

From Israel...

Dances the Hora. Smiles and bows.

From Greece...

Dances to Zorba the Greek. Smiles and bows.

From China...

Picks up mask of a dragon. Moves it around delicately. Smiles and bows.

(as LORENA) Look Ma! I fit!

Light change. Eerie sounding music.

A gang of kids waited for me in the schoolyard. "What will you do, now that
your leader is dead?" they rumbled.

I ran home in fear of what they might do to me and found my mother slumped
over the kitchen table crying.

(as Lillian) They shot him! The bastards shot him. They couldn't let an
intelligent Black man live. They couldn't lynch him, so they shot him. They
shot him! Martin Luther King! They shot him dead on the ground!

(as child) Oh, God! Our leader is dead, and my mother is moaning. I want to
stop her tears, bring him back to life, anything to keep my mother's strength
from crumbling before me. But she wasn't crumbling. She was angry, and the
fierceness she had always kept hidden from me was like fire in her eyes.

(as Lillian) Don't you ever trust the whites! Don't you ever trust them! Every
time you try to rise up, they'll beat you down again. They'll try to rob you of
your dignity. They'll try to steal your pride. They'll take everything you have in
this world just to keep you in your place. They'll even take your life. But there
is one thing God gave you that's yours to keep forever. And they can't take that
from you unless you give it up to them. I'm talking about your soul, Lorena.
Don't ever give away your soul. You hear me? I'm talking about survival in the
white man's world.

Don't let them break your spirit. Don't ever let them break you. If they knock you down, get up again. If they try to hold you back, just keep on pushing forward. Don't take no for an answer. Don't give up no matter how hard it gets. Just keep pounding on that door and some day it will open for you. Keep reaching for the stars and you'll have the universe.

We are coloured. And though your race will seem like a weight around your shoulders, don't let anybody tell you that you aren't beautiful and good. You are the future. You have a right to the future. Don't let anyone take that away from you.

(as child) There was conviction in her voice and determination in the lines of her face. The dream that was Martin, that light on the periphery of my existence, flares in the heavens like a star turned nova and shines on me from my mother's eyes. They may have killed our leader, but they haven't killed our hope.

> *White out.*

...Je suis perdue dans une plaine de neige aveuglante. Je mets mes mains au dessus de me yeux, pour les proteger du soleil. Je regarde autour de moi. J'ai besoin d'un repère pour me diriger. Mais tous ce que je vois est le bleu et le blanc du ciel et de la neige.

Je commence a penser que je vais mourir la. Mon coeur et mon corps – complèement congelé. Je vais étre retrouveé la bas, ou je me tient, dans cette posture, comme une sculpture de glace solitaire, exposé dramatiquement sur une couverture de neige.

Non. Je ne veut pas mourir comme ca. Il faut que je trouve le moyen de me sortir d'ici. Il faut que je bouge.

> *SFX – Aretha Franklin sings. "I need love, love, love." LORENA sings along.*

> *Slide – "Oh Mama. Is anyone ever going to love me?"*

(as Lillian) "There's plenty of time for that nonsense! You've got more important things to think about, like how you're going to get by in this world. If you spent more time worrying about your future than boys you might find yourself getting some place. And don't mess up your life by getting pregnant. Keep your skirt down and your legs crossed and stay away from white boys!"

> *Slide – "5 reasons to stay away from white boys."*

> *Jazzoid music. Upstage with pointer. Slide – a list which LORENA reads:*

1 – They only want one thing.
2 – They don't commit to black girls.
3 – They think all black women are whores.
4 – They make promises they can't keep
5 – They won't respect you.

But there are no black ones.

    Light change. Slide – "Amour."

He says he loves me but he won't speak English. He says, *"Je t'aime, Loren. Je t'aime."* I want to believe him. But my name is Lorena.

He says he loves me but he won't speak English. He's a *vrai* Péquist and won't dare to speak a word of the language of his oppressor. But the truth is my broken French is better than his English and I think it embarrasses him.

When we're with his friends, he speaks a rapid fire *joual* that's bewildering to follow. I try to nod my head and laugh in the appropriate spaces. But no one is fooled. Each exchange is followed with *"Comprends tu?"* Or explained in baby syllables – *"Il-a-dit-que-*blah, blah, blah. *Comprend tu?"* And sometimes when I try to contribute to the conversation, I'm told to, "Just speak English." They say," *Tu parle Français comme une vache Espanol."*

But when we are alone, his breath hot upon my neck, he murmurs, *"J'aurais toujours envie de te serer fort dans me bras."* I hear," I will always want that you claw hard in my arms." His words of love get lost in my kinky translations. Instead, I interpret the intimacy of his touch, the soft intensity in his eyes and abandon myself to the rhythms of his romantic language. I'm making love in French!

Then I understand that he will always want to hold me in his arms, because that is where I want to always be.

He says he loves me but he won't speak English. I turn to say I love you too. But check myself and say *"Je t'aime."* I want to say more but the words get scrambled in my mind. *Les mots ne viens pas facilement.*

    Slide – "Si tu veut parler Français il faut que tu pense en Français."

He says he loves me but he won't speak English. He wants to take me home. *A Drummondville, son endroit.* I don't really want to go. My love life is like the lyrics of a Janis Ian song. I know what heartache lives along that road. Still, we wind our way east along the St. Lawrence, through small towns with church spires gleaming white against a clear blue sky, meandering towards his history.

The farther from Montreal we travel, the more conspicuous I feel. I see surprise in the faces of diners in the Casse Croute in St. Hyacinthe, where we stop for lunch. Some sneak a peek at me between bites of hamburger steak and others gawk openly like I'm some strange and shameful beast. He is oblivious to my discomfort. Love is blind.

    SFX – Gilles Vigneault. Traditional Quebecois folk-sounding music.

His folks are of *vielle souche, les habitants,* sturdy, unpretentious folk. Their faces warm and open. Omer, with belt buckle lost beneath his *"grosse bédune,"* pumps my hand enthusiastically, *"Bienvenue, bienvenue!"* And Henriette, with her plain tanned sweater buttoned devoutly to her neck, takes my face in both her hands and presses her lips to my cheeks. *"Nous sommes trés content de te voir. Enfin. Marcel avais parl beaucoup de toi. Vienne. Vienne tassoire. Un place special pour toi."*

"Henriette don't speak no Henglish. Me? I don't speak good Henglish but I try."

"Comme vous voulez. Je parle Français. Pas tres bien, mais j'essaye aussi."

And we laugh.

I am surprised. They want me to like them as much as I want them to like me.

      Slide – *"Si tu veut penser en Français, il faut que tu vive en Français."*

He says he loves me but he won't speak English. Big fucking deal! I am elated. He says he loves me and he wants to live with me!

My Anglo friends complain they never see me any more. They feel betrayed. But they don't understand!

This language that I live in, this English I take shit for each time I leave my home, is not my English! Each word's a link, each phrase a chain that's forged in centuries of slavery. I speak Massa's tongue. And though I've mastered the language of my subjugation, I still yearn for the authentic voices of the lost generations of my ancestry. We share in spirit a desire to preserve what's left of our shattered identities. Side by side we'll fight the powers of oppression and live as revolutionaries in the struggle for social change. Together we will smash the shackles of colonial domination. Two niggers in America united by love. Free at last. Free at last. *Vive Quebec libre!* Free at last!

So I renounce my Anglo roots and move with him into a four-room flat on Colonial and Duluth.

We do the things that lovers do. Play in bed until two. Then crawl out into the afternoon sun, still entwined like differing plants that grow together – their leaves, a tangle of familiarity. Inseparable. Windowshop on St. Denis and browse in bookstores along the way.

This book is far from ostentatious. No bold print or glossy cover screaming for a sale. But sepia-toned and made to look like aged and faded paper. It is the doleful black face on the cover that rouses my curiosity and compels me to innocently pick it up and crack it's spine.

They say a picture's worth a thousand words in any language.

SFX – Faint southern gospel singing mournful underscoring.

It's not the smouldering remains of what had been a man that shocks me. His once black features charred beyond recognition. It is the twenty or thirty white men that stand behind the pyre, proudly arranged like graduates for a class picture. *(slides – close up on the faces of the men)* Their triumphant smiles. Their self-satisfied demeanours. Their total unconcern for the life they took, for that life was of no value to them except in macabre sport. Their shameless hatred. They didn't even bother to wear their hoods or robes.

Exposed and smiling for the camera, their eyes all seem to follow me. Pandora's book! I want to snap it shut but it's too late! I've been identified.

He says "Don't look. Loren. Don't look."

But I can't look away. I can't just look away.

He says he loves me. Even in English sometimes. His sudden fluency surprises me. But it really doesn't matter what language he says it in. Each time we pass that bookstore I have to stop and look.

Each time he says, "Don't look Loren. Don't look. Why do you 'ave to look at that?"

These men, these men who think they are so great, they are so much better, these men are everywhere! I have to remember their faces. I forget sometimes who I am and where I ultimately come from. These men remind me that a lapse of memory could one day prove itself to be fatal. And I want him to look with me. It is important that he look with me.

Regard, Marcel. Regard. Quelle sort des hommes peuvent faire ca!?

Slide – the complete picture.

He says he loves me. He says, "I love you Loren. I look at you and I see you. I don't see no colour. Just Loren. And I love him. Her."

I want to believe him. But I am more than the languages I speak. Who I am is embedded in every cell of my skin. How can he love what he can't see? What he won't see?

White out.

Light change. Hot, restrained jazz. Like the score from "The Pawnbroker." Dexter Gordon's "Tanya."

Slide – "The discovery of what it means to be a Canadian."

I was blind but now I see. I see it everywhere. In the eyes of the "other" that seem to look right through me as if I am not there. In the eyes of the dark and dispossessed, red rimmed with watery rage suppressed and masked with stoicism.

I see what my mother strived so hard to spare me, prepare me for. A world that's quick to judge a person solely on basis of the colour of their skin and not on their merit. A world where white is might and if you happen to be born Black – well, there's always room at the back of the bus otherwise, step down.

And this world isn't south of anywhere. It's north. True north. Strong and free. But for only the fair.

I walk...

> *Slide – "To be Black and enlightened in today's society is to be in a constant state of rage."*

...unemployed and almost homeless. Through streets of slushy grey, raining grey rain from a grey sky. Relying on the kindness of strangers and finding most are all too familiar in their response.

I see... *(claps hands and responds as if being slapped in the face)* why each apartment's just been rented when I show up for a viewing! I see... *(claps and responds again)* why the perfect candidate just precedes me at each job interview! Is it my stomach rumbling? Or the awakening anger within?

I walk...

Like a target though these streets.

Past scores of Haitian cabbies, fired from the SOS Cab Company for being what they cannot change... *(slide)*

Past three middle aged black women on their way home from church, being frisked by the police because they are suspect, suspected of being... *(slide)*

Past Anthony Griffin, gunned down by the authorities and lying in a pool of his own innocence and blood. *(slide)*

There's Ruben Francois,
Black Snow Goat,
waiting on the corner of Crescent and St. Catherines
with a can of gasoline in one hand
and a book of his self published poems in the other.
There's fire in his heart
though his smile is serene.

Anointing himself like Buddhist priest,
he calls to me...

(as Ruben) "When the weight of life is on your shoulder,
Sister, don't show any sadness on your face
for no one will pity you. Oh, look at me now! "

(as LORENA) He calls to me...

(as Ruben) "Get up and fight!
It's everybody's everything."

(as LORENA) He calls to me...

(as Ruben) "By God, I light the candle, burn the incense
the smoke in my head, a hole in my soul
proudly, walk I the streets in my search to be free
the spirit by my side, someday soon
you will know what I mean," he calls.

(as LORENA) Then sets himself ablaze in protest.

And I walk...

Past "white only" restaurants,
and "white only" taxi stands,
and "white only" apartment buildings,
and "white only" night clubs
and I see the unlegislated signs of segregation.
Subtle and tacitly agreed upon.
Unspoken
in two official languages.

> *Crosses upstage and sits with back to audience. Slides of Malcolm and Martin flash though fire. The music plays itself out.*
>
> *Light change.*

(as Ethel, the West Indian woman) I am tired, Lo. So tired of all dis French/English bullshit! Day in day out. Dey threaten' to close the hospital, you know? Notice is only the English one dey threaten. Dey layin' off people left and right. I lucky I still got me job. But I puttin' in double shift every other day. I so tired some days I just see white.

But I take every hour dey see fit to give me. I savin' my pennies. Because I know for you and me is not about French or English.

Here's what happened. I just finished putting in 11 to 7, 7 to 3. All I want to do is go home curl up in me bed ! But I got to take de boy to de dentist. So, I rush like hell from de hospital, grab de boy from his school and race clip clip to de dentist's office.

Now, I don't recognize de receptionist. But I don't pay it no mind. Dey change dese girls sometimes more often than dey change dheir undershorts. Dis one – skinny black-haired thing. She on de phone talking away and we stand standing dhere. We wait and we wait. Five minutes pass and we still standing dhere.

Finally she looks up at me and says,"What you want?"

I say, "We have an appointment at 3.30. Sorry we're a bit late."

She say, "That's impossible."

I say "What you mean I don't have an appointment. My name is Ethel Martin. It could be under my son's name Rasheed."

She say, "No. You have no appointment here."

Now me tinkin' what de hell's going on here? I take the appointment slip out of my pocket. I say, "But see. It's says 3.30. Monday. The 27th."

She say, "I told you. That's not here."

You know dhese office buildings everyting looks de same? De same white reception counter. De same orange chairs in de waitin' area. De same damn pictures of happy teeth on de walls! Noting but dis bitch to tell me is different. I was on de wrong floor. How was I to know dhere was another dentist directly below my own? I suppose I could have looked at de name on de door but I didn't. I was tired and in a hurry. It was a mistake. An honest mistake. Anyone could have made it.

So, me and de boy go leave and under her breath she says, "Stupid."

I don't know why I didn't let it slide. But I stop and turn around to her and I say, "You know. You are very rude."

And she come out from behind de counter, all red face, shouting, "You Black bitch! You get out of here!" And she shoves me through de doorway!

Now me feet ain't caught up wit' me body. I still got one in de office. She slam de door on my foot so hard de glass panel crack. And if dhat was not enough of an assault on my person, she follows me into de hall with her "stupid dis" and "Black dat" and "go back where I came from" and hitting on me and pushing me around.

I look at me boy. His eyes wide and shiny. I never seen him look so scared. He's moving back and forth like so. He's saying, "Mommy, Mommy lets go Mommy." But dis crazy bitch won't let me go. And then she turn and raise her hand to strike my child! Well, I just pulled back me fist and popped her one in de face. Grabbed de boys hand and went on about my business.

After his appointment, we step out of de building and dhat bitch is dhere wit' de police. "*C'est elle!*," she yells. And de next ting I know, I am being arrested for assault. Dey handcuff me hands behind me back like I'm some dangerous criminal. Rummage trough me hand bag. Feel me up and down so, like I got some deadly weapon up underneath my uniform. Right there on the street! And dey shove me and de boy in de back seat of de police car and take us to de station. All dat. All dat humiliation and degradation. Right in front of me child's eyes!

I don't go to court for a few months yet. You know dey wanting me to pay for de replacement of de glass panel dat bitch crack on me foot! De lawyer ain't worried. Plenty people waiting in the office. Good people willing to testify on my behalf.

But I tell you someting. When sis nightmare is over, I am packing up me things and taking me boy to Toronto. How can I teach him to have respect for people who have no respect for him. If is like dis now, what it goin' to be like when dey got dey own country, huh? I am forty-five years old. Ain't noting worth living out de rest of my life like shit on the sole of a Frenchman's shoe.

You damn right. I'm getting the hell out of here!

> *White out.*

Il faut que je trouve le moyen de me sortir d'ici. Il faut que je bouge.
Au loin, tres loin, il y a quelques chose d'a peine perceptible. Un tout petit point noir ou le ciel et la neige s'embrassent sur la ligne d'horizon.
Un tronc d'arbre peut etre. Un rocher.

Pas apres pas, je marches vers ce point. Mes yeux bas, ma tete baisse contre les lumieres du soleil. Je marche... pas d'empreintes dans la neige! Lentement, mais avec determination.

Il me semble que plus je marche, plus loin est ma destination. Que je ne vais jamais y arriver. Mais c'est du mouvement et ca me rechauffe et je retrouve mon espoir.

> *Light change.*

> *Slide/SFX – "Go..."*

We are sitting on her balcony at the Rockhill Apartments. The sun rolls down the slopes of Mont Royal cemetery and dances off the crystalline patches of melting snow, tender green shoots of new spring grass, and the glistening headstones of the gone but not forgotten.

Bundled like a baby in Hudson's Bay blankets, she complains about the cold and dampness. Despite her discomfort, I insist that we stay outside for a little while longer. She rarely leaves the apartment anymore and needs the fresh air.

Slide/SFX – "Go..."

You would not know that she is fifty-seven to look at her. She still looks like she could be my sister and I am the youngest of five adult children. It is her hands reveal her true internal age, which is about seventy-five. Her clothes disguise the rest.

Slide/SFX – "Go..."

These hands.... These hands have large mis-shapen knuckles and fingers that are crippled, bending at the joints every which way. Her "zeds," she calls them in an attempt at humour. But mostly she tries to keep them hidden from view.

Slide/SFX – "Go..."

I drop to my knees and rest my head in her lap. And despite pain I know she feels, she takes one of these hands and smooths back my hair, caresses my brow.

I say," Oh mama is anybody ever gonna love me."

She says, "I love you."

I say, "Oh, Maw. That's not what I mean."

She says, "You have plenty of time for that nonsense."

I say, "You've been saying that to me since I was fourteen years old."

She takes a lock of my hair in her crocked fingers and tickles my ear. Like when I was child and she wanted to wake me. But I am awake and a woman now.

Slide/SFX – "Go..."

I say, "I've been thinking, Maw. Maybe that person that's meant for only me isn't in Montreal. Lord knows I've worn my heart out searching the city for them. Maybe they are somewhere else in the world. Just waiting to meet me. It's possible."

"Anything is possible, she says. "If you believe."

And one of these hands attempts to squeeze my shoulder reassuringly.

I say, as conversationally as possible, "You know Lisa's gone to Vancouver."

She says, "Uh huh..."

I say, "Yeah. Louise is in Ottawa. And Brenda just got this great job in Toronto. Pretty soon I won't have any friends left at all."

"Have you found a job yet?" she asks.

"No." I say. "But I am okay for a few months. Something will happen soon."

And for the longest time these hands sit silent and heavy on my shoulders...

"Go," she says. "Go to the farthest place. And work your way back. If you have to. You can always come back if you have to."

But how in good conscience can I leave these hands? These hands that slapped and nursed me? That played "Moonlight Sonata" and delighted in braiding my hair. These hands can no longer carry a Steinberg's bag, button a blouse, pick a dime from a change purse or brush her still black and lustrous hair. These hands. How can I leave these aching hands? How can I leave these hand when they obviously need me so?

As if reading my thoughts she says, "As long as I am here you will always have a home to come back to. So go. Go. Don't worry about me. I'll be just fine. I have survived this long, haven't I?"

I put my arms around her waist and bury my face in her her lap. The oesteo-arthritis is all through her body and it pains her to be held. But she endures my embrace. I smell her through the blankets. The smell beneath her perfume. Her smell. I love her smell. How can I leave her smell?

She pats me on the back and laughs, "I'll help you pack."

And then these hands release me. Like a thousand yellow butterflies fluttering goodbye.

White out.

The sound of an airplane. Raises an umbrella.

Rainrain rain rain rainrain rain rain rain rain rain rainrain...

Dear Louise,

Greetings from soggy Vancouver! It has been raining for eight days straight and the streets are covered in slugs. Brown slimy things, not unlike long runny turds that ooze along the side walk. The streets are just slithering with them. Really gross.

I can't believe it's been three months already. It feels like for fucking ever.

I have moved out of my sister's windowless basement in Surrey and into a one bedroom apartment in the downtown west end. There's nothing in it except my bed. But it's three blocks from English Bay! And I have developed a fondness for sitting on the beach and "watching the ships roll in." Just like in that Otis Redding song. Yes girl, Lorena on the beach! I'm doing nature! You can't avoid it out here. It's fuckin everywhere. Mind you, I am going to have to get appropriate footwear. My heels keep getting stuck in the sand.

I got myself a little job at an all-night *depanneur*, excuse me, convenience store about four blocks from where I live. I had a job in market research but I got fired when I didn't show on June 24. I said, "Hey it's St. Jean Baptiste Day. A holiday." They said, "Not here it ain't." And gave me the boot. It's just well. I was getting tired calling people and asking them intimate questions about their feminine protection.

How's Ottawa? Capital punishment? I don't know about you but I am finding it hard adjusting to life in Canada. First of all people don't know how to dress here. Everyone looks like they just crawled out of a kayak or some other outdoorsey thing. Bush bunnies. They wear big cloddy boots all the time. (The better to stomp slugs with I guess.) I find I am overdressed for just about every occasion. And I can't even dress properly because there's not one place in the whole fucking city that sells flesh coloured pantyhose the colour of my flesh! I won't even talk about make up or hair products.

There are no Black people in Vancouver. I can go for days where the only Black face I see is my reflection in a store window. And when I do see one I stop and try to flag them down.

Everything shuts down at 1am like some fucking temperance colony. You can buy pornography at the corner store but not beer and wine. (Figure that one.) And people get in your face for just about everything; for smoking cigarettes, for swearing, for waving your hands and raising your voice when you get excited. Don't get passionate and above all, don't get political. It's like there is some law against having fun here. The B.C. No Fun Laws. They are really frustrating.

And English! Its so omnipresent! Did you you know that the STOP signs actually say STOP!? In big bold white letters?! And nothing else!? Is it like that everywhere in Canada? Everywhere uni-lingual English signs. It's creepy.

And I don't understand this English. Back home, you were Italian, you were Greek, Polish, Hungarian, Dahomian, whatever, you spoke English it was an agreement. A way of establishing common bonds. You were a part of something. It made you feel like a revolutionary. But here they use it to bludgeon people with. Particularly immigrants. They say, "You're in Canada now. Speak English!" And there is actually a group called "The Society for the

Preservation of the English Language." It's probably just a bunch of old Brits sitting around eating mushy peas and singing "Rule Britannia." But still, it's offensive. I feel like I just traded one kind of language prejudice for another.

I got a call from Peter. He's thinking of moving out here. And you remember Leslie? She lives just two apartments down from me. I keep running into all kinds of folks from home. Every day there's a new batch of refugees. French and English. It's funny, in Montreal none of us would give each other the time of day but here – we cling to each other. Here's a gang of about twenty of us expatriates. We get together every so often to eat and a drink and smoke and talk and swear real loud. Hell, we even speak French and we don't have to, anymore. We go to restaurants that promise a taste of home. Montreal style bagels and Montreal style smoke meat and Montreal style barbecue chicken. We have come to the conclusion that there's a pokey little town somewhere in Missouri named Montreal, cause we ain't et anything in Montreal, Quebec that tastes this shitty.

The one thing we've learned living here is that we may speak all English, but we're sure as hell not Anglos. No matter what Bourassa or Pariseau or any of them say we are Quebecois. And we each feel out of place in Canada, in our own way.

I miss Montreal. And I want to go home. But can't cause I promised my mother I'd give it a year. 3 months down, 9 to go. Meanwhile, rain rain rain rain rain rain rain.

Write soon. And if you get back to Montreal, tell her I love her.

Your friend,

Lorena

P.S. I almost forgot. I met a man.

> *Light change.*
>
> *SFX – Voiceover and kookey laugh in style dance music:*
> *"Steamies at Montreal Pool room.*
> *Smoked meat Schwartzes.*
> *Schullers kosher Barbecue potato chips.*
> *Cotts Black Cherry soda, cause if it's Cott it's got to be good!.*
> *Dry garlic spareribs at the Dragon Inn on Decarie.*
> *Cream cheese party sandwiches from the Snowdon Deli.*
> *Orange Tarts at Café Castillo on Sherbrooke by The Cinema Five.*
> *Sunday brunch at les Filles du Roi.*
> *Praline and Ice cream crepes at Le Petit Halle.*
> *Hamburgers and french fries at Lafleurs.*
> *The lobster festival at Amazona's on Cote St. Luc.*

Bagels from the Bagel Factory on Fairmont
Pineapple chicken at Lung Fungs.
BarB Barn Ribs.
A Cabane a sucre *breakfast with scrambled eggs bakes beans, back bacon, home*
fries, and tortiere.
Chicken at the Chalet Barbecue.
Onion Baji's at the Star of India.
Blueberry cheese cake at Le Commencal."

Live.

I crave the flavors of my past and must taste again the city that I love to eat.
I will devour Montreal, savoring each sweet and sour memory that bursts upon
my tongue. I will dine at eight, and until three, I'll gorge myself with reverie
and laugh again with those I loved!

I'm going home. Home. Where the heart is. Where the hate is. Where the
have to, hard to, happy to is. The prodigal daughter returns with a hunger.

SFX – Voiceover:
"Chocolate cake at Fridays.
Pendelli's Pizza.
Coquille St. Jacques and profiteroles *at Chez Delmos on Notre Dame.*
Three fish terrine at La Rapiere.
Hot polish sausage at the Cafe Prague."

Light change. Slide.

6180 Durocher still stands.
And though the filmy white curtains
have been many times replaced
with those of other styles,
by those of other tastes,
the long glass door panels
still gleam
invitingly.

I dare not ring the bell
and ask to mount those steps
again.
I've crossed that threshold many times.
Let other lives
play out their mundane dramas
between those walls.
I am content
to stand outside
imagining
the secret and familiar spaces

I once knew
to be mine.

    Slide.

Schwartzes is still packed
and spicy smelling.
Pickled peppers,
medium fat
double mustard
greasy fingers
slipping
on the cold tin
of my black cherry pop.

    Slide.

And lunch at Chalet Barbecue
is still the cheapest deal in town.

But Cafe Prague... gone.

    SFX of projector but image comes up empty. Repeated throughout this section.

Dragon Inn – gone.
Star of India – gone.
Cafe Castillo – gone.
La Petite Halle – gone.
Lung Fung's – gone.
Finast's – gone.
Franks – gone.
Strathcona Academy – gone.
Guy Drummond – gone.
Each pilgrimage finds that mecca's disappeared
without a forwarding address.

    Slide.

St. Catherine Street feels empty.
The hollow-eyed store windows,
once dazzling with bargains,
Now stare blankly behind
À louer and
à vendre
signs.

    Slide.

I stand
on the corner of Peel and St. Catherine
at 5pm on Thursday
waiting for the light to change
feeling cramped
by the buildings
that I'm seeing for the first time
without
their payday crowds.
I cross the street
alone.

Slide.

I delight at finding
Grumpy's
still downstairs.
But my once nightly retreat
no longer feels jazzy
nor exclusive
with it's pub style
renovations
and my booze buddies have all
moved on
in body and in spirit
or aged
beyond my recognition.
I drink a toast
to the echoing
"last call" laughter
of my past
and leave
drunk
with disappointment.

Montreal and I have changed.
She does not bear
the weight of
her depression well.
But sags
like baggy stockings
around
an old woman's ankles.
And I have become accustomed to
green
Westcoast surroundings.

"Go to the farthest place
and work your back...
if you have to.
You can always come home...
if you have to"
my mother said.
Even she is gone.

Light change. Slide – Joe's. Sits and talks directly to audience.

And this is what I was going to tell my friend before I was so rudely
interrupted. I had gone to Montreal to visit my mothers grave. It had been
three heartbroken years since she died. I needed, not only to make my peace
with her, but to make sure that she'd been buried in the right spot.

You see, my mother never liked the heat. And some graves are right out
there in the open. I didn't want her sweating in the sun for all eternity. So
I specifically requested a shady plot beneath the tree. But she died in January.
The tree was naked and spindly. And I guess the ground was too frozen to turn
because when I left the cemetery, her casket was still sitting out on one of
those portable folding tables on the spot designated for her burial. The ground
hadn't even been broke. For all I knew she was still sitting out there.
I needed the closure of seeing that she had been committed to the ground.

Now, my mother was buried in Memorial Park Cemetery in Ville St.
Laurent. My friend Andrew offered to drive me. And though I had the
vague recollection of the cemetery being on Cote de Liesse just past the
National Film Board, I thought to check the address before we left.

So I look in the White Pages and it's not there. I look in the Yellow Pages and
it's not there either. I think okay. You're in Quebec now. Translate. I look under
Parc Memorial. Nothing. Cemetaire Memorial Nada. I call the information
operator and she insists there are no such listings.
Now I am really in a panic. A whole fucking cemetery can't just get up and walk
away! Where the hell is my mother!!?

We hop in the car, drive up Cremazie, onto the Metropolitan, exit on Cote de
Liesse and... bam! The one-eyed guy and the NFB are right where I remember
'em. We drive a little further and come to the high stone walls of the cemetery.
It too is just where I remember it.

I'm thinking, "Now, what the Hell just happened there?" Maybe the cemetery
just got filled up and stopped advertising. We'll drive up to the gates and see a
red neon sign flashing "No Vacancy" or "Standing Room Only."

We see a sign all right and it is not amusing. It say's Les Jardins Urgel Bourgie.
Les Jardins Urgel Bourgie! That's no translation for Memorial Park! Les Jardins

Urgel Bourgie! It's an Urgel Bourgie Cemetery! They sold the fucking cemetery to Urgel Bourgie!

Urgel Bourgie is a large French undertaking company. My mother hated them! She always said "I've had to live my life in French. I want to die in English. Stick me in an English cemetery like Memorial Park. And no matter how cheap it is, don't let those Urgel Bourgie people touch me!" And now she's decomposing in the shadow of their sign. I hear cursing in her grave.

They could have informed me of their intent to sell. I would like to have had the chance to voice my opinion on their decision. Or, at least given my consent. But this was decided independently of me, like so many decisions being made in and around Quebec.

I found my mother right where I left her. Only six feet under. And it was as I requested – a quiet shady spot beneath a spreading maple tree. I sat for a moment and contemplated her epitaph: "Too well loved to be forgotten." I noticed at least a half a dozen other grave stones in her immediate vicinity that bore the same inscription. There must have been a sale that year. "Too well loved to be forgotten."

Aw, ma. How could I ever forget?

> *White out.*

Je retrouve espoir. Et soudainement, ma lueur est la, en face de moi.

Ce point sur l'horizon blanc, n'est pas un rocher ni un tronc d'arbre. Mais une femme, noire et completement nue dans la neige. Je ne peux pas voir son visage son dos est tourné vers moi. Mais je sais qu'elle n'est pas aveuglé par les lumieres ni géné par la froidure.

Elle se tient toute droite sa tête haute et fière. Ses mains placés hautainement sur ses hanches, et ses pieds plantés solidement sur la terre. Elle a l'air complètement chez elle, indifferente a cet environnement hostile.

Qui est c'est femme qui defié les elements et ose revendiquer cet endroit pour elle?

Je m'approche lentement d'elle et pose ma main sur son épaule. Ma main tremble. J'ai peur. Elle se tourne vers moi et je realise alors... qu'elle est moi.

C'est moi!

Et je me reveille.

> *SFX – "Une Quebecoise Errant."*

On October 30th, 1995, I felt as if I'd come dangerously close to being severed from both my personal and family histories. And Pariseau's remarks regarding "pur laine" and "ethnics," made it clear that the years and generations my family has invested in Quebec were perceived to be of no consequence or value. We would never be accepted as Quebecois. Because we are Black and English-speaking, I did not have the right to love Quebec, to speak to that love, or to vote for it.

When I moved to Canada I did not stop being a Quebecoise. I discovered that I had always been one. I did not forfeit my identity. I gained it.

I am expatriate anglophone, Montrealiase, Quebecoise. These are just a few of the memories of a life I lived in the land of my birth. I cannot be separated from them. They cannot be legislated out of being. Nor can the Supreme Court rule on their validity. They are a part of the distinct whole that is me.

Memory serves me.
An exile
in Canada.

The end.

Alien Creature
a visitation from Gwendolyn MacEwan

Linda Griffiths

As playwright and actor, **Linda Griffiths** is the winner of five Dora Mavor Moore awards, a Gemini award, two Chalmers awards, The Quizanne International Festival Award for *Jessica*, and Los Angeles' A.G.A. Award (*The Darling Family, Alien Creature*). Her plays include *Chronic, Alien Creature, The Duchess: a.k.a Wallis Simpson* and *Maggie & Pierre*. She is the co-author of a unique theatre book – *The Book of Jessica* (co-written with Native author and activist Maria Campbell). Griffiths has created collective work (*Paper Wheat, Les Maudits Anglais*), and has published short stories and poetry. Her company, Duchess Productions, develops and co-produces much of her work, as well as producing a unique playwrighting class – Visceral Playwrighting. A partial anthology of her work, *Sheer Nerve: Seven Plays by Linda Griffiths* is available through Playwrights Canada Press. Her next play is based on the Victorian novel by George Gissing, *The Odd Women*.

Alien Creature: a visitation from Gwendolyn MacEwen is a winner of the Dora Mavor Moore Award for Outstanding New Play, a Chalmers Award (2000), and a Governor General's award nomination.

Alien Creature: a visitation from Gwendolyn MacEwen was first produced by Theatre Passe Muraille in association with Duchess Productions in the Theatre Passe Muraille Backspace, November, 1999, with the following company:

GWENDOLYN   Linda Griffiths

Director/Dramaturge   Simon Heath
Lighting and Environment Design   Jan Komarek
Stage Manager   Beth Brown
Creative Consultant   Sandra Balcovske

First published in 2000 by Playwrights Canada Press.

Characters
— —•— —•— —

GWENDOLYN

Playwright's Notes
— —•— —•— —

This play is inspired by the life and work of Gwendolyn MacEwen. But there has been double inspiration, first from MacEwen herself, and then from the extraordinary biography of her life by Rosemary Sullivan, *Shadowmaker*.

Anyone interested in MacEwen's love of magic should read *The Magician*, and *Carnival*, both found in the anthology, *The Early Years*.

There are thirty four lines of Gwendolyn MacEwen's poetry in *Alien Creature*. Everything else in the play is new material. Then there are other poems. Not hers, mine. I can only describe them as "theatre poems." I start writing the script and these poems come out, little rhyming pieces that said a certain thing I needed to be said at a certain time. So presumption of presumptions, there are these theatre-poems mixed in with the poetry of this real poet. How do I explain?

I want to address this to the people who knew and loved her and tried to help. I want to say, "This may not be your Gwen, or you may find glimpses of her when you least expect it. Then there might be times when you think, 'she would never say that.'" The person that is present that you don't know is me. She and I are doing this play. And only both of us can speak.

— —•— —

In the original production of *Alien Creature*, magic illusions were used throughout. Later we found it was possible to perform the play sitting on a chair with no movement and no physical magic at all. Most of the stage directions involving the magic have been removed from this version in order to free the reader's imagination...

Alien Creature
a visitation from Gwendolyn MacEwen
— — • — — • — —

In the darkness of a space in limbo, the shadow of a woman appears. It is as if she has been called up from some other dimension. Gradually she begins to appear more tangible. She walks forward towards the audience as the light around her brightens. She stands for a long time before speaking, looking at the audience, as if drinking them in.

Gwendolyn

You're so beautiful. You look like great bunches of black grapes, you look like "renegade electrons searching for a core," [1] you look like moon striped pieces of... sorry, it gets to be habit. You look like... people sitting in an audience. You're very precious to me. You came. So I feel I have to warn you that I do die in the end, so things might get a little intense. I hope you're not afraid of excess. But I did not commit suicide. I drank myself to death, it's different. Don't Sylvia Plath me and I won't Sylvia Plath you.

Excuse me, I think I have to throw up. Nothing personal.

When I used to do poetry readings, backstage I would be vomiting and retching up whole gobs of entrails and blood and old women would come and read the future... no, not true. But I would vomit. A small Canadian wren shaking with fear. And then I would come onstage and something would happen. I would become taller and broader and wiser. More beautiful, more powerful, more... pure.

There aren't so many of us now, there used to be hundreds of thousands. You'd see fifteen at one party. Something has thinned down the ranks of those magic women, alien creatures, some but not all dark-haired with regular features and some great bead around their necks. A genocide of floaters, of mythopoeic sluts, paddy wagons filled with wisps of girls in trailing velvet tops clutching cheap Tarot packs. I never really liked the Tarot. They tried to kill us and I totally understand, my only question is why they bothered. They came with their calculators and merging endless mergers they got so powerful, but how were we dangerous? I still see some on the streets, disguised in smart outfits of all kinds, I want to go up to you and say, "I know and it's all right, I won't tell anyone."

I'm sorry! I didn't mean to frighten you. Damn those creative sparks.

I always used to want to get shot. You know what I mean? In the right upper arm. Right there. I wanted to grit my teeth and say, "it's only a flesh wound." And then save everybody anyway. It's only recently that I think, what a totally stupid idea. It's bananas, totally bananas. I don't want to get shot. It's just that sometimes you want a chance to be heroic against something as tangible as a bullet.

I want you to know I was brave. I want you to know I fought hard. I want you to know I loved beauty, that I laughed. I want you to know I was a coward. I wish... I wish.

I see a billboard, aimed at the young. It says "Too soon old, Too late smart." Ignore it. Come into my place. Mind and heart.

> *Behind GWENDOLYN, a golden light becomes brighter and brighter, illuminating the brick walls and the high windows of a basement apartment like no one has ever seen before. There is a chair in the corner. An old trunk. Lights dance over the space.*

Come into my beautiful basement,
and you'll never think of mutual funds again,
nor will you think of business zen.

I have a genius with small spaces
I've done great things with all my other places

> *From the trunk she pulls out a red cloth trimmed with gold, an exotic pillow, a bottle of Russian vodka and a glass.*

I'll light candles on a trunk
That's filled with iridescent junk
The trunk is covered with
a wondrous cloth,
sprinkled with ultraviolet moths
the cloth
is sometimes a curtain
but that's not always certain,
sometimes the cloth
covers pillows
then the cloth,
becomes the moth.

Come into my beautiful basement
and we'll laugh
And have fun,
shoot arrows at the sun.
Time for dreaming and seeming
dancing like bulls teeming
with fertility and waste,
come into my place.
Make haste.

I need a drink. Vodka, a woman's drink. Colourless, odourless, so it almost doesn't exist.

"Finally then do all my poems become as crazy scarves
issuing from the fingers like a coloured mesh
and you, magician..." [2]

My mind is filled with shards of ancient pottery, with bits of lapis lazuli, with cups from Mycenæ... my mind is filled with bullshit. Oh yes, those magic women, all through the ages, mind filled with bullshit magic women, they have that otherworldly look at least when they're young. And they either get settled down so you never would have known they were ever like that, or they become strange and wounded and get too many cats. Like fifty. I know, I know. I don't want to be like that anymore, I'm taking up a career in sales.

And why not? I watched this city get sold.

I hated this city because it was unmagical, it tried to kill the surreal. It was hogtown, circled with slaughterhouses, a place of diligent, unimaginative commerce. But something was going on, something exploding, the hogs were squealing and squealing, the pigs were all over town. Oinking our way into a culture. And then, something changed. A breath of air, a piece of falling mortar, the smell of sulphur, and all of sudden the house I was living in was worth double what it was worth the previous month and then triple what it was worth the previous four months, and then five times what it was worth and ten times what it was worth and the ground I was walking on was suddenly worth more than gold and I looked and saw we were scattering to the corners, all the poetic piglets were running to the basement hovels of our city. Oink. The very ground had shrunk.

I don't want to be poor. I don't like the idea of being poor. Just because I'm a poet doesn't mean I don't like light coming through the window like anyone else. How did it happen? Did they suddenly put a circle around and we were on the outside?

The city will pay! The city will pay, the world will pay! For every poet forced underground, for every painter even if the paintings are stupid, for every possibly, no probably, pretentious artist forced to flee, there will be payment, maybe not this year, maybe not next year, but in the foreseeable future, all of us, all of you are paying!

Oh yes, this city is as divided as Jerusalem.

I'm sorry, I don't mean to go over the top. It's just that the top is so low these days, all you have to do is be standing up and you're over it.

What is it like now to be young and luminous? Do they take you in? You think it was hard then, back at the beginning of it all. But it was easy to be nineteen and luminous and about to be published. I could be taken in because the few there were, were so lonely. There was nothing, almost no novels almost no poems, it was a desert, and you could be Lawrence of Arabia taken in by the local Arabs, or in this case, the Protestants.

There were warehouses as big as pyramids, you could hide in them. Your ancestors are hiding there. Go on. Talk to them. I'm one of them. Make me an ancestor of this city...

I thought the clock wasn't ticking, I thought we were trying to find a fourth dimension and wonder of wonders the fourth dimension turned out to be stocks and bonds.

Their Global reach is murder, their Global reach has no language, has no Gods. My Global reach is full of broken tongues, at least I speak them. *(Arabic) Ana Alemt Naffi Arabit*. Come out. I see you, hiding in catacombs, winged feet in black boots, wearing chains and the piercings of slaves, come out.

I don't mean to poor-mouth. I have a reputation, I can wrap that reputation around me like a forest-green velvet cloak. The kind magic women always seem to want to wear. And I knew. I always knew I'd get to do this thing and I have gotten to do this thing. When you change your name at the age of twelve from Wendy to Gwendolyn because Wendy isn't the name of a serious person, you know.

I'm five years old, maybe younger and there is soft rain. For some reason I'm dressed to go to church or have gone to church and the world is holy and heightened. I'm alone on the street there's a laneway or a path, no, because I can glance over and see our house, but the trees form an arch over me and drop warm rain on my new coat. I reach up and pull off a few flowers, hold them in my hand, walk down the archway like a nun, like a bride. I am dedicating myself to something and in the air is honeysuckle. I think I'm dedicating myself to God and maybe I am, it was to some higher force. I said, "I am your bride." And so many times I have felt bound by that vow, times I've thought, "What am I doing? Why am I killing myself writing poetry?" And I think of the silver grey of that moment, of my child self exalted with holy self-importance. Some god is there, and sacrifice, glory if anyone is watching, and the sense of doing ultimate good. Where is that bouquet of honeysuckle now when my bank account is empty and my body full of pain? Tiny flowers, not showy really, a golden, tawny colour, a strong sweet smell and my young soul singing.

GWENDOLYN's hands begin to shake slightly.

There's something I have to tell you. There's a condition that happens sometimes, not when you drink, but when you stop, called Metabolic Acidosis. I never wrote anything about Metabolic Acidosis, I'm afraid she has halitosis... the body becomes so used to receiving certain fluids, that when you stop, it can create convulsions, epileptic-like seizures, heart attacks. Not from drinking, but from stopping drinking. Stopping dead. That is what is about to happen. But not yet. Poetry is breath, and sometimes the breath comes too fast and sometimes nothing at all will let it in.

Last night I had two green peppers for dinner. Fried. And a big bottle of vodka. And then I drank and read comics all night. The Marvel Family is so prosperous. Then around four in the morning a Jack Palance movie came on TV.

Maybe I didn't mention that I am besotted with Jack Palance? The actor who does the one-armed push-ups? I just love that man, he looks so squashed. His nose has been broken so many times and he's gentle and fierce and he has a ranch and horses. "Body of many wings, beloved, body of many blue wings." [3] I don't want you to think I'm angry. I'm not. I love living inside this mind, it's a constant adventure. Me and Jack Palance and the horses and the archways. They used to laugh at me reading comics. I read them long past the time when you're supposed to stop. Wonder Woman. Wonder Woman was a suck and a slave. She never sold very many comics, but I needed her. She had a bad hair-do and a stupid skirt, the skirt looked American, like she was wearing a flag. But her mother was an Amazon, strong and proud. Amazons were created from the great cosmic maw of reborn souls. In the comic the souls look like a lot of paisley shirts in the sky. And Zeus comes down and says, "I will create a new race and that race will be female."

Many years pass and then all the signs are clear. A Being, a titanic energy force of great evil is chained deep beneath the island of the Amazons, and it is rising, refusing to be calmed. The date has been prophesized since the beginning of time. It is the Eve of Destruction. Wonder Woman, who is a suck and a slave, has somehow lost her lasso, but she has a helmet with plumes and breastplates, she wears the silly skirt, and carries a golden spear.

All the Amazons are watching, because she is the chosen one. Chosen to save the universe and all the gods. Her mother doesn't want her to go. The earth shakes as she enters the first cave. Many things befall. There are eyes in the dark, spears come at her from every direction, traps, the ground gives way under her feet, flames that shriek go past her head, at one point everything is flame. You see beads of cartoon sweat on her face. She is looking for a monster. Then she's in a cage. Like a shark cage, each bar is made of intellect, each bar a language, each bar an iron concept. The cage is lowered to the very centre of the earth where no one has ever gone before. And she finds herself... in a nursery. It's so sweet and pink that she is lulled into opening the door of the cage. Where is the monster? Where is the thing that's going to cause such destruction? Then she sees in the corner a filthy creature sitting in its own shit. The smell is enough to make her wretch, there are no superpowers to keep her from gagging. She can't tell if the creature is male or female, hair covers it's warped body, she sees long talons, catches a glimpse of fangs. But she has pity for the creature, it's alone, frightened, it looks at her with eyes full of tears. It's a child! And Wonder Woman is filled with sorrow, she reaches out to touch the matted hair. The creature grabs her! And Wonder Woman struggles with the creature, it's on her back, between her legs, sucking her breasts, inside her mind. She knows it is not her strength that will save her, the creature is stronger than she is. The cage of intellect is behind her the door is open, if she can get to the cage the cage will save her and the creature knows it too. Then the strangest thing happens, she starts to fall asleep. Even as the creature and its poisons burrow deeper and deeper inside her, she feels like curling up into a nice little ball, feels a warm blanket put over her, and a sweet song sung to her.

(*singing*) You're nothing but a nothing,
A nothing, a nothing.
You're nothing but a nothing.

You're not a thing at all.
Not a thing at all....

I can't find a way for her to win. It is the creature who is stroking her long black hair. And she is sleeping, sleeping...

But that's no way to sell comics! And so what happens is, with a mighty feat of strength, courage and training, Wonder Woman throws off the creature, stabs it with her spear, runs to the cage, sees the creature is wounded but not dead, closes the door, hears the shrieks of the creature. The Eve of Destruction is put off for another thousand years. The cage rises, she goes through the caverns and tunnels, exits the final cave. She doesn't know if she can walk but she does, bleeding and victorious. Her mother embraces her and a great cheer rises up from the Amazons.

No one notices the shadow of the creature following behind her.

But that's not modern. Gods and Amazons, not modern. You have to disengage to be modern. And what you have to do to be post-modern I've never figured out. I wrote a book. And it's so good. Every poem. Not a clunker in it. Boom and boom and boom and deeper and darker and lighter and funnier. There. How much is that worth? That's what I said to the bank manager when I asked him for a loan. There, how much is that worth? He was under the impression I would be late for our appointment. I said, "I am always on time for deadlines, and furthermore, I've supported myself as a poet for twenty years without a day job – running IBM would be a vacation." No, that's not what I said, that's what I wanted to say. I doubted. I thought, "you're a fool. You're not trying hard enough. Where are your RSPs, where is your mind? You could learn Arabic, you could learn Hebrew, you could learn Greek, ancient and modern, why couldn't you get together a simple down payment for a house?" I rallied. To show him my yield potential, I marched home and brought my twenty books, plunked them on his desk and said. "I did these, how much is this worth?" He looked at me with these quite lovely blue watery eyes and said, "nothing." The Truth. I kissed him on the mouth. He looked very surprised. I don't think anyone had ever done that after being turned down for a loan. I gathered together my twenty books in two shopping bags, walked out of the bank, muttering ideas for a sequel to the *Odyssey. (Greek) An boro na miliso ten glosa tote boro na chorepso to choro.*

I had long since left off wearing my long velvet robes, I was dressed in a lumpy wool coat and winter gumboots. I know what people saw.

I could do it if I wanted. All I'd have to do is make a certain shift. And the phone would always be ringing, and my assistant would be in the other room making coffee. Herbal tea. And I am in a perfectly cut business suit. The kind magic women always like to hide behind.

Gwendolyn MacEwen, Poetry International? I told you, I want John Cassavetes to do the film. He's dead? Well then get Quentin Tarantino, just tell him he has to use Jack Palance. Two hundred and fifty thousand, no negotiating...

Not convincing yet? Like a child playing? I'll get better. A conquistador of modern business. Gwendolyn MacEwen, Poetry International? Not enough. What do you think they want in L.A. these days? Poetry. Poetry. Poetry. They can't get enough poetry. Gwendolyn MacEwen, Poetry International. You want a jingle for a one shot yeast infection pill? Well, you could always go, "super-cali-fragilistic-vaginal candi-dosis." Poetry International. Sarah would you come in please? You're fired.

Hire five more. Yes that's five. Poetry International?

GWENDOLYN's father's voice.

"Gwen, I want you to know how proud I am of you, honey, you've done so well. You know I don't like asking but, would you have a twenty till I get my welfare check?"

Dad? I'll write you a poem. Something soft in a big raincoat. Poetry International. Nono no no. I'll be in London, then Athens, then Rome. Poetry International. François, *comment ca va? Midi Mercredi, Salut.* Poetry International?

GWENDOLYN's mother's voice. A voice from hell.

"You fucking cunt! I saw you on Queen Street. I saw you spreading your legs for men. I saw you..."

Mom, can I call you back in five?

I know there's a middle. I know that flipping between extremes is not a good idea, I know there's a sacred little path between the two. "You have the Jekyll hand, you have the Hyde hand." [4] My therapist was blind. They gave her to me for free. In the corner is a seeing eye dog, a beautiful German Shepherd. "We have to get to the bottom of the well. We have to go right to the pit of the pain. It will take time and patience. You have to come every week." But she didn't come every week did she? She disappeared. "I'm leaving a message for Gwendolyn MacEwen. Gwendolyn? You missed your appointment. Gwendolyn? I haven't seen you in a while. Gwendolyn? Gwendolyn? Gwendolyn?"

Her mother was mad
and her father drank.
So sad. So sad.
Her mother was sad
and her father...

Whatever you do, don't write poetry.
I mean it.
It's bad for your... liver,
it'll make you... shiver,
it bloats the bladder,
it sads the sadder,
and bads the badder.
It causes osteoporosis,
it makes more hair than usual
grow out of your... noses.
For the females
a dreaded mustache grows
and that's in addition to the hair in the nose.
Fur balls
coagulate and furbulate
in the small intestine
Do you think... I'm jesting?

Then there's the flappy thing
under the chin, the colostomy bag
smelling of old pee
old pee...
is that really me?
And all from Poet-ry?

I have to stop all this rhyming
and metaphorizing
I'll tie myself up in ropes, chains,
finally use some brains...
or... manacles
wrapped round my clavacles...

GWENDOLYN grabs a pair of heavy steel manacles. She walks into the audience, manacles in her hands, and asks one of them to lock her up.

I am going to need some help. And then I will eat a very large bowl of... kelp. Actually it's you I'd like to tie me in chains, then maybe I can borrow some of your brains. It's very simple, just take the lock, I'm sorry, I just really have to stop. Don't be afraid to snap it tight, it's so important for me to get this right. Now the other side, I hope you don't think I'm taking you for a ride. That's swell, you are helping me out of a kind of hell. Oh, that's so much better! I'll have to write you a... card.

> *GWENDOLYN, stands in the middle of her audience and rattles her locks and chains.*

This is so good. I'll never get out. Poets are magicians without quick wrists. Well, no more poetry for this girl. I can feel myself becoming more tangible by the moment. They'd never let me into the fourth dimension done up like this. Think prose. Think filing. Think flossing. Think faxing.

I'll go back to the bank manager as a real person in the real world...

> *The manacles suddenly drop to the ground with a giant thump. GWENDOLYN stares at them on the ground.*

Shit.

"silent as Houdini who could escape from anything
except the prison of his own flesh." [5]

Poets love the dark. Drunken clocks,
electric gardens, kindled children, strange breakfasts, rattlesnake spines...

Her mother was mad
and her father drank.
so sad.
Her mother was bad
and her father... blank.

What's in the house
on top of the hill?
Madness.
Murder and madness on Keele St.
The murder of tender things.
What's in the house
With the crooked stairs
And the attic so high?
A madwoman's cutting
A vein in her throat,
And her daughter won't even cry.

What's in the house,
On the top of the hill,
daughter?

You're performing a trick. First you are wrapped in an old-fashioned straight
jacket, the kind they used to use for murderous criminals. Then you are placed
in a glass coffin, maybe like that guy in New York, and the coffin is placed in a
water boiler, and the water boiler is placed in a tank, and the lid is nailed shut.
And you know the trick, you've done the trick a thousand times, but this time
you can't get out. You're looking for some image that will set you free. The air
is running thin, everyone is watching, the coffin is real, and you are locked,
locked in a thousand chains. Where is that image? "Everything dies and I'll get
God for that." [6]

Poets love the dark. But what does that mean? What's your dark? Is it lurid
bodies being eaten by worms? Electrons like mad bees circling your head? Is it
germ warfare? Going blind? Waking up paralyzed? Excruciating pain? Your
mother dying? Your child dying?

The child I never had was mad.
Red and hoarse, even coarse,
It was unnatural and bad.
A twisted lump, with eyes that burned red
And almost no head.

So when they ask me about the child I never had
I never say, madness skips a generation
I never say, what gives you consternation
Is that I never had the child that was mad
Never.

Poets love the dark. Then there's a moment in a sun-filled kitchen, I don't
know why I say "sun-filled" because I lived in so many basements. Someone is
standing there, maybe it's a man, so like another man, and unlike, that you find
yourself sinking down into some realization you don't want to have. About your
life. About repetition. About friends and cycles. The moment makes you sick.
You fight it, you don't want to feel it. It hurts. And yet you allow yourself to
sink right into your guts. Not for yourself, but for the poem. And the poem
may or may not be dark, but the moment is always dark. It's always dark to go
somewhere you don't want to go.

Someone you know hangs themselves, do you imagine the rope, the body
swinging, of course not... unless you're moved to write a.... Do you find out that
at his feet were four cigarette butts? Do you imagine him smoking them before
he did it? Do you wonder if it took a long time to die there alone in the woods?
Do you wonder if he got an erection at the last? A big blue one. I have a sense
of humour. The dark doesn't.

I want to offer you my dark. Take my dark. Please. Take my dark. A joke. "Together for one second we are light." [7]

If I were to say to you, I've had many lovers, I think I'd be giving you the wrong impression. Not that I haven't had many lovers, not that I've ever counted. But to say, I've had many lovers is to present myself as a bit slutty maybe and it wasn't like that. I've been married more than a lot of people. Twice indeed. The first I won't talk about, there are too many rumours. The second I wore the veil. I took the vows. And I'm still very connected to him. The one where I wore the veil. But in between and around what I'm trying to say is that I lived in a world that was voluptuous. Where the meaning of sexual contact seems different from now. I loved all of my lovers. Loved them. Loved them. And they loved me. And when we made love, we were learning. It was the kind of thing where you could say, "sex is my sacrament" and no one would snicker. I'm not saying living like this doesn't have any problems. I'm not saying there aren't children left over from that time knocking on doors, asking, "are you my mother?" But I do believe that some things go hand in hand and when the language of this lovemaking left, something else left too.

I wonder if I was a good lover. I'd like to think so. I'd like to think I gave something, that there was a weight to it. So I can say I've had many lovers just like I can say I've had a lot of cocks inside me and I have. There are times when I think I can't stand to have one more cock inside me. Not one more. No. Go away. And so to say I've had many lovers is also to say I have paid a price. Then there are days when I sit back and smile. And I think of all the men and all they gave to me. And not just the entry in the night, but the play of it. And because I knew how to play, I think maybe I was a good lover. And if things got a little tortured, things got a little tortured. We're not supposed to love drama, we're supposed to love reality. I never understood that.

I've been thinking about the heart. My heart. How it pains and twitches sometimes. My heart is in a cage and my ribs are that cage and the bones are torqued and twisted. The idea that you're supposed to give your heart. Such a simple thought. And I lay beside him that night and thought, "my God I've got to do it again."

I've been thinking about the words, I love you. How often with my little loves, with my many loves I've exchanged those words. To say they're tarnished would be an understatement. And I've thought they could never be said again, not by me to anyone, not by anyone to me. And then I see you. Yes, you. Don't be shy. Mr. Sensible. No, you don't have to say anything, I actually prefer my men not to speak English. Your eyes are so clear, not poisoned at all, you must drink a lot of water. I'm looking for someone to keep my Lord Death from the door. Is it you? Let's break plates like the Greeks and dance on the shards, never cutting our feet. Let's make love in the park and shoot arrows at the moon. Let's stay up all night and.... Oh, I know. Do I want a woman like that? Men like peace, I understand. I can't offer you that. But I can offer you nights of wonder.

I reach into my mouth, down my throat, around my lungs, push aside my breastbone and pull it out. And in those minutes, hours, weeks, before, I know if you will replace it with your own, I stand in the world, heartless.

> "Poetry has nothing to do with *poetry*
> *Poetry* is how the air goes green before thunder
> is the sound you make when you come and
> why you live and how you bleed
> and the sound you make or don't make when you die." [8]

It's coming back. I've seen you as I've walked these streets. Tiny dark rooms and bars are filled to the rafters with poets. It's the Eve of Destruction, there's a lot of rhyming going on. A slithery kind of rhythm, hypnotic, then razor laser sharp. Too many leaping words to lock up. They will take to the gardens and alleys of the world, these poets, or they will shrivel in the septic sun. Come out. I see your eyes gleaming. Come out. Speak to me of victory.

(Hebrew) Gam hosech lo yahsikh mimeka v'layla qa'yom ya'ir, qa'hesheikha qa'orah

> "We all have second degree burns
> And they hurt but the hurt doesn't matter.
> The living flame of the world is what matters." [9]

It's dangerous. I'm not saying it's not dangerous. The travelling is definitely dangerous. You can start to live in ancient places so an electric light bulb looks indecent and cars rather cruel. There are days when I pick up a telephone and I'm shocked there's a voice speaking to me. There are days when I'm struggling to open the plastic wrapping covering a box of crackers, when nothing at all seems to be able to break it, and I think, "how did something so strong and foreign come into my world?" There are days when I wander the streets as a stranger and an exile and all the electronic waves in the air become absolutely too much to handle, and things are too bright, too loud, too fast to last. Poetry is the fastest thing I know, but it's not that other quickness, that deadly speed.

I bang into this acquaintance, I wouldn't call him a friend, and he says he has the flu, and so does his wife and kids. He says, "It's a bad time for families and the flu." I say "I had the flu."

It was then that I realized I hadn't been invited to dinner in six years. And I didn't understand why I had just slipped off the edge of a world where a hundred loose acquaintances lived. People I knew almost well. Certain kinds of people, people with cars. And I thought, am I a dud at the table, is my conversation less than sparkling? What am I, chopped liver? They go quiet and act like they're being kind, they wouldn't want to bore you with talk about their children in the face of your exciting single life but really it's a primal act of condescension. You can talk to me about anything, why not your children? Then I realized it was starting to show, like a dirty slip hanging below my out-of-fashion skirt, like the bruised mask of the sick. It was starting to show, at writer's gatherings where there are thin crowds and a lot of standing. Poor thing, only forty-six, she's looking so old, on the sauce again. Slurring her words. They ask her the future and the hag says, "I know, I'm just not telling anyone." No, you don't want her sitting at the table. They think I just write sad stuff. I do not write dark fluff. Why is she ruining the neighbourhood with all those cats? They're protesting at the abortion clinic, but they don't care about the animals crying for water. Ask me a question. Ask me a question. Okay maybe some people still called, and I didn't call them back, maybe I don't want to go out with them anyway, maybe I'd rather go out with George the rubby. George knows how to have a good time. He doesn't write poetry and he hasn't had a bath in a long time. Who was it that hadn't had a bath in a long time? Oh right. My first husband. Shhhhh. I wasn't going to talk about him. Not a word.

We were married for five months. Five months. And no one ever forgot it. They blame me still. I was nineteen, that still counts as a teenager. He was forty-two, it was a mistake. I don't want you to think I'm angry, I'm not angry, but... hell's bells. How would you like to be part of a couple called beauty and the beast? Insulting to both of us. I was no beauty, just all young people are beautiful, and was he a beast? Was he a father figure? Yes. Was he a brilliant poet? Yes. Did we have wild and crazy times together? Yes. But you couldn't talk to him, not like a real person. He was a great raving entity. He was a stinky man. Have you ever been with a stinky man? No, I'm sorry, you'd remember if you had. Oh, sometimes it was hard. Stinky men know damn well it's hard. Their smell is a gauntlet to the world. Go away, here is my smell. Come here, rise above my smell if you are true. Love me, for my wounded animal smell. And I did. But I began not to be able to breathe. Poetry is breath, I couldn't breathe. I tried to explain. And then one day you're in the kitchen screaming, "you stink, you stink, you stink!" And you know what he said? "It will always be a problem." And then you saw the beast for he sank his teeth into me and wouldn't let me go, howling to the world about betrayal. I married and loved for a time a grand stinky man and he sent his scent after me till the day I died.

At first there are wild dreams, world domination, a line of t-shirts, thousands coming to your door, leaving flowers on your stoop. I'm published in the States, and I am twenty. If there's no money, there will be money. If there's never any money, I'm just fine about that. It's not about fame and money, it's about the words coming out. And the world is this big. And the ground is this big. Then the circle gets a little smaller. The good publishers turn into bad publishers and the cover photo makes you look like a dweeb. And you sell less copies than expected even though everyone says... the next publishers are smaller. Fine. Work. Work hard. And there's a little less money. And it's more difficult to find a place to live. And you almost get raped in Jerusalem, you come back and the circle seems a little smaller. There's a grant, but the grant doesn't quite cover what it was supposed to cover, and no one's reading poetry any more, but they think you're just so wonderful. And the bottle is bigger as the space is smaller. You say, "All right. It's stupid, world domination. Those were young thoughts of fame and bullshit. All I want is to do good work, have some people read it and a basically full belly." No. Fine. I'm not going to argue. I don't expect special treatment just because I write poetry. Work, work hard, and I'm old and the world is reading even less poetry and that's just fine. I'll write a novel, there's no need to be bound by poetry, and the novel is about someone with no identity lost in a land as big as the sky, but it's too specific or too general, there's something wrong with it, something wrong with me. And the circle gets a little smaller. You say all right I won't expect that, I won't expect to write novels and make a killing or anything like that. I just want to write poetry and have that poetry get out. No you don't get that. You get the basement. And the circle gets a little smaller. And you quit drinking cold again and start to have convulsions, they take you to the hospital and your friends ask, "Is she an epileptic? We always knew she was touched by the gods." And the doctor says, "no, she's a drunk." And the circle gets a little smaller. And no man and no children and the fire is taking up all the room and the work is going well and I've written it all and there's two dollars in the bank and a green pepper for dinner and the circle is so small... until you're dancing on the head of a pin.

They're announcing me at a reading at the Club Bamboo, my twenty published books, my awards, my alien dignity, and I come out...

Don't look at me don't look at me I don't want you to know where I live you can't cross that line over there I don't want you to look at me don't poetry is breath poets are magicians without quick wrists poets are poets are breathe in and out breathe in and out wait...

(Mother's voice) You fucking cunt! I'm going to kill myself because of you. I don't want daughters!

(Father's voice) Come here, Gwen, come here, don't look at her. Let me hold you. Come here. Let me.

(Mother's voice) Get away from me! I'm going to slash my throat because of you. Blood everywhere because of you, daughter.

(Father's voice) Gwen. Come here. It's all right. I just need a drink. Don't look at her, I just need a drink, then I'll hold you, I just need a...

> "It is moving above me, it is burning my heart out,
> I have felt it crash through my flesh,
> I have spoken to it in a foreign tongue,
> I have stroked it's neck in the night like a wish." [10]

Don't touch me!

> "Beware! I now know a language so beautiful and lethal
> my mouth bleeds when I speak it." [11]

My blind therapist said, Gwen, you have to find more joy in your creativity. Joy. Yes. Deep inside. With my poor art and imperfectly I have wept fire, I have surfed subatomic mist, I've raised desert Queens, I have ridden ancient battle scenes, I've stitched up continents on my sewing machine. You can't begin to know the joy I feel in what I have done.

But.

You try and you try and you try and you write it away and you laugh it away and you fuck it away but it comes back and back and back. No, you don't get that. You get this. You don't get that. You get this. And then there are no poems there is no fire there is no breath there's a weight and a shadow. There is nothing because you are nothing.

> *(singing)* You're nothing but a nothing,
> a nothing, a nothing,
> you're nothing but a nothing
> you're not a thing at all
> not a thing at all
> not a thing at all.

And even then, you think, there's a way out. There's an escape. There's a way out there's an escape. The trap gives way under your feet the basement is at the very centre of the earth but you think there's an escape there's got to be a there's a there's an escape there's a.... Here's an escape.

He's cold. Cold eyes. He's not your lover. He is your constant companion. Every night around four in the morning, you hear him knocking.

And you say, "Thanks, not tonight." And he replies with elaborate courtesy, "Very well, Gwendolyn. Tomorrow then?" "Tomorrow then." There are no footsteps when he leaves. If there was just one poem left inside of me I wanted to write. Then when he came knocking, I would say, "Sorry, I'm working. This nothing is putting out another silly poem. Pretending she's important. Believing she's important." And that would keep him away for a while. I could go over there and write one more brilliant poem, but why?

So this night when he came knocking, I answered the door, invited him in, offered him a seat on the pillows. He's over quick and sitting down. "Would you like a drink?" I offer. "Why don't we drink what I brought?", he replies. It looked like vodka, except it's a strange colour of violet. His hands tremble slightly as he pours it into glasses that come right out of his leather jacket.

"Shall I put on some music?" I said. "I'll play myself," he replies. He takes out a gypsy violin and plays beautifully except icicles hang from the bow. I was careful never to look into his eyes and he knows it too. "I seem to have lost the taste for poetry," I said. "Really?" He replies. "How very sad." "But I haven't lost the taste for this."

Still I didn't drink. "Funny, I was a howling maniac just a few minutes ago and now it's like we're having a party." "It is the Eve of Destruction, a party to end all parties." Still I didn't drink. I smelled. Oh you've never smelled a drink like the one my Lord Death brings to the door. Sweet and fiery. The whole world went violet for a moment, as if it was being covered in cellophane. Coated. He was smiling so lonely like a child I knew what had to be done. "I'm sorry, I would like to invite you to stay, and have a lovely time, but I've decided I'm not going to drink tonight." He looked very grave. "Have you forgotten the pain?" I smiled, "Oh, I'm an expert on not forgetting the pain." We both knew what was to come. He rose with his exquisite politeness, even made a courtly bow. My hands were already starting to shake, but I think I hid it well. As I walked him to the door, he paused, trying one last time, saying with great tenderness, "Why choose such a fate when one small sip with me...." I was tender too. I knew his lips would taste like sand. "The next time you come, you'll have to break down my door." With that, he was gone.

I'm sorry, but I did warn you.

> *In silence, GWENDOLYN kneels behind the trunk, packs her things and goes to stand. Almost imperceptibly, she loses her balance. She steadies herself. She seems confused, as if she doesn't know how to get back to the trunk. But her arms reach up to close the lid, the fingers white as light.*

I want you to know I was brave. I want you to know I fought hard, I want you to know I loved beauty, that I laughed. I want you to know I was a coward.

"I swear by all the famous, ancient lions I have known
That the mighty children yet to come
will foster finer stars,

For they are the true lords, born of morning, whose coming will call us down like a deck of cards." [12]

> *The lights begin to fade as GWENDOLYN smiles.*

"I am starting to haunt you. I am starting right now." [13]

> *Curtain*

> *The end.*

Translations
— — • — — • — —

Arabic. Pg. 92.
Ana Alemt Naffi Arabit
I speak Arabic

Greek. pg. 95
An boro na miliso ten glosa tote boro na chorepso to choro.
If I can speak the language, then I can dance the dance.

Hebrew pg.100
Gam hosech lo yahsikh mimeka v'layla qa'yom ya'ir, qa'hesheikha qa'orah
Darkness is not dark for you;
night is as light as day;
darkness and light are the same.

Gwendolyn MacEwen's Quotations/Poems
— — • — — • — —

The following are the quotes from the work of Gwendolyn MacEwen that have been incorporated into the text of *Alien Creature*. All other text is by Linda Griffiths. Permission for use of all quotations from the work of Gwendolyn MacEwen has been granted by the author's family.

1. Renegade electrons searching for a core.
    "The Names"
    Noman's Land

2. Finally then do all my poems become as crazy scarves
    issuing from the fingers like a coloured mesh
    and you magician...
    "The Magician"
    A Breakfast for Barbarians

3. Body of many wings, beloved
    body of many blue wings.
    "Blue"
    Afterworlds

4. You have the Jekyll hand,
    You have the Hyde hand.
    "The Left Hand and Hiroshima"
    Breakfast for Barbarians

5. silent as Houdini who could escape from anything
    except the prison of his own flesh.
    "The Magician"
    A Breakfast for Barbarians

6. Everything dies and I'll get God for that.
   "Dark Stars" -
   Shadowmaker

7. Together for one second we are light.
   "Marion Marini's Horses and Riders"
   The Poetry of Gwendolyn MacEwen:
   The Later Years

8. Poetry has nothing to do with poetry
   Poetry is how the air goes green before thunder
   is the sound you make when you come and
   why you live and how you bleed
   and the sound you make or don't make when you die.
   "You Can Study It If You Want."
   Afterworlds

9. We all have second degree burns
   And they hurt but the hurt doesn't matter
   The living flame of the world is what matters
   "Second Degree Burns"
   The Fire Eaters

10. "It is moving above me, it is burning my heart out,
    I have felt it crash through my flesh,
    I have spoken to it in a foreign tongue,
    I have stroked it's neck in the night like a wish."
    "The Red Bird You Wait For"
    The Shadowmaker

11. Beware! I now know a language so beautiful and lethal
    my mouth bleeds when I speak it!
    "But"
    Afterworlds

12. I swear by all the famous ancient lions I have known,
    that the mighty children yet to come will foster finer stars,
    for they are the true lords, born of morning,
    whose coming will call us down like a deck of cards.
    "The Lion"
    Afterworlds

13. I am starting to haunt you
    I am starting right now.
    "Past and Future Ghosts"
    Afterworlds

Getting it Straight

Sharon Pollock

Sharon Pollock's works for the stage have been produced throughout Canada and around the world. She is the recipient of numerous awards recognizing excellence in drama and is a two-time winner of the Governor General's Literary Award for Drama for her plays *Doc* and *Blood Relations*, with works translated into Japanese, Dutch, French, and German.

Other stage plays include *The Komagata Maru Incident*, *Generations*, *One Tiger to a Hill*, *Whiskey Six Cadenza*, *Death in the Family*, *Saucy Jack*, *Fair Liberty's Call*, *Walsh*, *Getting it Straight*, and *The Making of Warriors*. Her recent collection, published by Playwrights Canada Press, *Sharon Pollock: Three Plays*, includes *Moving Pictures*, *End Dream* and *Angel's Trumpet*. Ms Pollock resides in Calgary, Alberta.

Getting it Straight was first performed at the International Women's Festival, Winnipeg, Manitoba, July 1989, with the following company:

EME   Sharon Pollock

Directed by Rick McNair
Set design by Linda Leon

First published in 1992 by Red Deer College Press in the collection Heroines: Three Plays. *Reprinted with permission.*

Characters
— — • — — • — —

EME   a woman dressed in an eclectic blend of clothing one might find in a bin at the Goodwill store. Neat, pressed but well-worn, a bit of a fight between stripes and checks. A hospital plastic identity band on her wrist.

Getting it Straight

— — • — — • — —

*Light patterns reflect what may be bars, ribs, open seating, the exterior structure
of a grandstand, as seen from the inside out. The patterns shift and change,
perhaps as a result of the sun rolling round the Milky Way, the earth swinging
round the sun, the moon moving round the earth, or perhaps as an external
manifestation of the electrical impulses inside EME's head. She is hiding under
the grandstand in an area used for storing incidentals and where a certain
amount of garbage has also accumulated.*

Eme

robin   robbin'   robinrobin robin
robin in the rain what a   nasty   fella robin
   in the rain   digging   for your breakfast

with your   long   strong

beak
somewhere
someone is looking
checking
checking the ladies somewhere someone
is
beneath
under here quiet here still
now I say
are there others?
looking like
others
no others
maybe others
bootsmell of, leather copper, smell of blood, salt
taste of tears, you smoke rag ends!
Shhhhhhhhh
I say, just to the ladies
they say, right back!
I say
fine I lied
calf's neck snapped back with rope small children
little
britches! one event only!
come on! come on yah come on gerry! chute 5 on
white devil! jerks and twists like a metal toy made
in taiwan that I find in my stocking and wind with a
key I say this is no kind of place to take someone

like me on a pass!
even I know that!
I have no hat
for one thing
I say just to the ladies then I go down go under
they sit
excepting for freida?
no
they sit
eyes focused on horse with eye bulged out strap
cinched tight rider's face pocked like the badlands
spasmodic like
myrna
they say too much medication not enough medication
myrna's eyes roll up showing
whites riding white devil!
then
I find my way under or
it finds me I say here is a secret here I think
here is a good place I think
of ubu roi of the nightmares of the blind of the nut-
cracker suite turned sour I think
of a very large collection of string puppets
hung
in a very small
room
backstage I think
of mime
and
panto-mime
and of
mirrors and of
wings
I think of the layman's guide to schizophrenia and of
ubu roi
again but I remember camus! I think
of
brown skin and tubercular chests and smallpox
blankets bought from the bay I say
how did you get here?
I think of giants and
of animals that speak and of people who remain
silent I think of cassandra turned inside out I think
of cat scans of the brain of satellite photographs of
the earth I think!
of real
and
unreal

shuffled
like a deck of cards play the hand I say!
they say
another sign
shadows
of a violent mind I see
white rain
garnet red the clouds I hear
the floating world it sighs
a little sigh they say I'm mad
I say enola gay little boy fat man!
little boy little boy fat man!!
Shhhhhhhh be quiet stupid
I think
of
getting it straight I think
it began as a headache came on
just
after the news sweaty hands
pounding heart accompanied by
feelings of apprehension diagnosed as
a case of tension do you ever ride the bus watch
the news read the papers magazines books look at
people's faces! oohhhhhh lungs labour mind races
stop clock freeze frame cover story?!
they say
I'm mad I say
you know what I say
they say this
is paranoia this
constant growing fear of hostile forces that
threaten to destroy me advertently or
inadvertently covertly
or
overtly should death
dressed in a mushroom cloud or
strangely mute fall from the sky burrow in
they say
you can do it tinned food and bottled water will see
you through it, that and a good spermicidal jelly
they say I'm mad I say little boy little boy fat man
fat
i
isee
icey the woman the woman
I see the woman
who
washes

the floor in our ward cleans my toilet picks up the
pieces I rend and tear little pieces my hands won't
let go I!
see
a boat
that lies dead
In the water I see
it burning I see a small burning boat on the immense
blue ocean under a cloudless sky split!
split
by the tiny plume of black smoke which drifts
drifts from the burning boat I see it on the 28 inch
screen of a tv set with the sound turned off
help me I say!
I think of the earth like a bell the slightest
touch
sends tremors resonating round its surface the
woman
shows me
a small
photograph
of
a
family
on a saigon street they say
I dreamt it I say
getting it straight freida says
where would they get a camera?
this seems an odd question to me
maybe I dreamt it I
IIIIIII
iiiiiiiiiiiieye
I was always close to my father!
loving my father!
yes these are the kind of questions they ask you
here, are you close to your father?
yes
what do you call him?
daddy no not daddy father that's what I call him
father
they say his name?
they say his name?
I say r.d.
the initials you know that's
him
r.d.
I say
his father died 2 months before he was born

they want to know these things so I
say my father was the youngest in a family of 13
yes the youngest child and the only boy yes 12
older sisters and him the only boy he
didn't
talk or say a word until he
was
almost 4   I say
maybe he had nothing he wanted to say
I say maybe he had a lot he wanted to say but no
one would let him say it!
I say r.d.
they say but
what is his name?
I say, when
I was little
my father took me aside and he told me
r.d.?
a mistake
had been made yes he
says his mother my gramma,
you know
post
pression she couldn't
fill
out the forms
well you can't take him home they said no one it
seemed worried about her depression it was her
fear of paper
concerned them but it's all right I say he says
he tells me when I am little
the nurse will fill out the forms
the nurse will fill out the forms
these things happen
his mother my gramma says
artie
not arthur but artie
she
was very particular about that, not arthur but artie
you can't call him that says the nurse!
why not says gramma
because
it's a
diminutive!
nickname!
nickkk! says the nurse
artie says gramma!
you can't call him that says the nurse! was the

nurse confused? gramma was depressed but even
depressed my father's mother was Formidable!
the nurse filled out the forms
but not artie no not artie at all
r.d. I say all a mistake right there on the form I say
my father confided in me me loving my father when
I was little
these are things believe me they want to know
I say he
has no idea how his mother found out what she felt
like why she never did change it no idea at all
life is like that
the nurse was confused
or malicious
my father never knew no never knew no never even
suspected his name wasn't artie till
labour day
labour!
day the following day to be
his first day
of school when someone
some person or
some group of persons
probably female
slipped a note under the door of his room
I say his mother and him?
they never discussed it I say
his 12 older sisters and him?
never discussed it
he lost the note
I say
do you think he could have dreamt it?
they say
nothing so
I
zip my lips
and I dream
I dreammmm
I lie on my back in a field full of yellow mustard at
midnight
I look deep into time for the nearest stars are tens
of thousands of years closer than the stars that are
distant and far
time
being space
being time
my room
is square 1 second by 1 second when I run

screaming rushing hit the wall pressing in small
7 seconds by 7 square measured walk drift
in a dream
sloow
space stretches
like vowels,   roooooooooom
grooooows I see
the milky way holding back the night so that
fragments of black are unable to fall crushing me
and the mustard and
a very small egg
that I hold in my hand it
could crush
you too
like an egg
they say–
I say
nothing
I whisper
I'm not certain if I dream it or   if it dreams me
they say
nothing useful
I think, they will check the forms for my father's
name
I laugh!
I say, my grandfather rides a camel across the gobi
with polo
he is a man loves travel he maps the water web
from the rockies west till the land runs out and
stranded he stands on a strip of sand his eyes set
on a golden ball sliiiding down the pacific he
is a travellin' man rides a rocket to the red star
is a man loves puttin' space between him and
where he last slept loves
looking out
into time my
grandfather
works for the railway sells tickets in a rust red
station house 4 seconds by 3 with a potbelly stove
and the smell of creosote filling the air
measure
the dimensions of my grandfather's life by
economic circumstance standing behind a wicket
selling tickets to other travellers he only travels
in dreams
when
he
retires they give

him
a pass, he is an old man then, I sit on his knee
this is the way the farmer goes this is the way
the gentleman goes this is the way the lady goes
boom! fall in a ditch!
he hides
his top plate in his hand then he smiles and I scream
and we
laugh
inside
my grandfather's head a black hole blossoms in the
shape of a rose, he thinks of the gobi, the pacific,
and mars, he
boards the train in winnipeg for the sault but gets
taken off in
thunder bay he boards the train in winnipeg for
drumheller but gets taken off in swift current he
boards the train but
my father
always
calls ahead my father
visits my grandfather on sundays I
go along
for the ride I sit
in the parking lot with
the top
down
on the car I
look up
at the windows the faces of young men cross
hatched with wire look down I say
ollie ollie oxen all outs in free!
I say ollie ollie oxen all outs in free!
the black rose
blooms in my grandfather's head he escapes!
riding a swollen petal like a flying carpet leaving
an empty shell in the corner
of his cushioned room
I sit on his knee
and he hides his teeth
boom! fall in a ditch!
Shhhhhhhh under is safe is it safe? Shhhhhhhhhh
listen
whoop
whoop
whoop of siren flashing eye push!
freida falls
floats feet

together arms
outstretched mouth an empty ooohh and a look of
surprise in her eyes
this seems less real yet I have a small stain on my
skirt there
are things
I cannot bear to think about I see
enola gay on the nose of a plane written by a midwest
american hand wielding a russian sable brush!
enola gay?
a short woman
whose hair has gone quite grey
the colour of her eyes?
faded
washed out by some internal bleach enola
drives the pickup out to the field with lunch
scans the sky for rain, snaps a photo of a
prairie sunset, sends it to her pilot son in the
pacific is immortalized on the nose of a metallic
bird does
enola see white rain garnet red the sky does
she hear the floating world sigh its little sigh?
enola?
enola you answer me!
hear me enola gay!
weather
means a lot to prairie people
claude
eatherly
flew lead plane he
only checked the weather
it was good
he gave the sign
claude eatherly
being most sane
went insane
they say
I watch too many specials I
hear
the voices of students calling for their mothers and
at the base of a bridge inside a big cistern that has
been dug out I
see
a mother weeping
and
holding above her head
a naked baby
that is burned bright red all over its body and

another
mother
is crying
as
she gives her burnt breast to her baby and in the
cistern students stand with only their heads and
their hands above the water and they
clasp
their hands
together and they cry out
calling
for their
parents but
no parents come and every single person who passes
is wounded
all of them and
the
hair
of the people
is singed and frizzled and covered with dust
they don't appear to be human
they don't appear to be creatures of this world
I have children
where are they?
I have a stain on my skirt
maybe
his sister has them
or my mother where are your children who has them?
returned in a green plastic garbage bag or walking
north from the pas till the cold sets in? don't think
about that standing in a lineup for stamps it's hard
not to try telling people that they say
try a little rolfing jogging gestalt
try a little est and sex and tai chi
try a little acupuncture
meditation maybe try that
try alcohol
try politics and prayer try a sauna just relax
organic food
sometimes that helps
try 2, 10 times a day the bottle's big and it's
refillable try an institution try a smaller room try
insulin
electric shock try
deprivation try
alienation try
hallucination try
isolation they say! this is schizophrenia this

psychotic disorder characterized by delusions
withdrawal deterioration and violent violent
violent!
my children
have grown and my mother is old now so
she said
you do well in math, eme, excel
in
things mechanical like change the oil and washers
for the tap she called that mechanical she worried
I'd never catch a man
you'll sit at home you'll be alone
I caught a man!
I sat at home
I was alone
myrna
myrna's caught 3 men
that's irresponsible myrna
myrna says for better or for worse
myrna never says for good
why don't you just shack up with them?
myrna says it would upset her mother
your mother's dead myrna!
myrna says she doesn't want to take the chance
myrna
shoots the pills up her sleeve like a card shark
later she will chew her tongue in a feeding frenzy
myrna says at home she has a dog that growls,
a fireplace that smokes and a cat that stays out
all night, so now she doesn't need a man
I laugh
she likes that
she whispers I'm seein' someone and he makes
in the neighbourhood of a million bucks a year
I say that's a nice neighbourhood
what'll you have?
well what've you got?
myrna drinks anything that pours but
most of it she spills on her shirt
the tv is suspended high in a corner of the ward
in a wire cage
we could play a game
but
all the parts are missing I see the disappeared I
hear the dispossessed I know we can read a
magazine you know the one with all the pictures
of the women
who have made it

to the top it's all the rage turn the page
glossy photos of their children
very clean
and smartly dressed smiling
spouses country
houses and a long shot
of
some art I lived in a house in the country I lived in
a house in the country my brother bubu and eme and
mummy and daddy and me lived in a house in the
country bubu
is
bubu is
42 when? what? now! 42! my mother always calls
him bubu he likes it
she cuts his meat
he lets her games aren't that important eme
he lets her games aren't that important eme
let bubu win the game tonight he sleeps in the same
room he
slept in
when he was little he sleeps in
the top bunk he keeps
his papers
in the bottom bunk bubu bubu has 3 degrees and the
only way bubu could win a board game is by divine
intervention
games aren't that important let bubu
win the game tonight we lived
in a house
in the country I
see

(sings) shutters green shutters
yes shutters and shade
I see the shutters
and lacework of shade
green wooden shutters
darkening shade
my heart is aching green shutters and shade
emily emily emily emily emily emily em

(speaks) we picked

(sings) berries red berries
yes berries and bark
I smell the berries
warm sunlight and bark

brown bitter bark
my heart is breaking sweet berries and bark
emily emily emily emily emily emily em

(speaks) bubu and eme eme and bubu ollie ollie oxen all outs
in free run! run! ollie ollie oxen all outs in free!
bubu!
how do you get from there to here?
spring forward fall back   have
a coffee?
cream?   no cream have a sugar? no
sugar
nutrisweet?   petroleum
product powdered in a brown jar with coffee? and
the radio on top of the frig hap hap happy jack
and his cock a doodle doo crew down at click
wishing you and yours a hap hap happy hostage
takin' in beirut bush threatens to nuke nicaragua
to teach iraq a lesson I've had it up to here says
bush hemorrhoidal relief for pennies it can be yours
with financial terms you can afford am I on the air?
right now I'm on the air?
they're in the air!
the word is out the back pack nuke is in
ideal for bridges dams and similar installations
with a slightly larger model in the works for cities
over 60 thousand easy transport in compact car or
truck yes truck pack tightly
in one container
two slugs plutonium with explosive
good ole country billy on your country billy station
with I'm pinin' in the fallout of your heart good
pickin' on mass murderer in moose jaw pleads
justifiable homicide on 22 counts of
do you think thermo underwear would help in a
nuclear winter or should you stay with wool and
other natural fibers? send 10
superpowers threaten war over grammatical error
in diplomatic dispatch today
the dow jones reports today
we have the means to erase iraq from the face of
the earth today
we turn baghdad into an inlet today
a child died today
they say forgive your enemies
today I forgive a few of my friends today they say
they want 2 megatons he gives them 2 they want 2
thousand they get 2 thousand it's just a job the

corporation's into everything today he says technician
misreads metric radioactive release today I want to
ask you
if you don't have a basement or a shelter would just
closing the window help? I open
I
open I open
his briefcase and I it's late at night and I
I am making
cookies?
for
something
yes, for something at school, career day at school
role
models are assembling in the elementary school gym
at 8:30 for 9:00 and my job is to assemble bake
and convey along with the children some appropriate
bars
booth bay bars
a creative extrapolation from mummy's nanaimo bars
I open
his briefcase I read
his papers I read
things that
disturb
me I burn
the bars I
shut
the briefcase I
assemble
more–
when he leaves in the morning he carries the
briefcase it hangs from his hand he looks
different
I
drive
the children to school along with some
squares
I say
what are you going to be when you grow up will
you grow up going to grow really up?
yes these are questions that begin to concern me
now I
watch the news look in books ask around exploring
their
options to see
what they can be when they grow up also so they
can answer the question everyone asks after they

say you've grown you know the what do you want to
be one and I
find
an interesting thing did
you
ever hear of
hypatia?
she's a physicist
yes that's the one
mathematician astronomer philosopher and she is
beautiful and she never marries and her father's
name it
never said! and there is a man and it says his name
and his name is cyril and he hates her
physicist mathematician philosopher science and
love no! not that word other words freida
says
take it with water and
cyril and cyril and cyril and his friends and yes he
has friends and they seize hypatia and they throw
hypatia down and they have sharp shells abalone
shells and they skin her alive and they throw away
the work that she's done and she is forgotten and
in
time
cyril
is made
a saint I
think
they want to be cyril getting it straight this frightens
me I
say nothing
say nothing shhhhhh nothing at night
we lie together no not together we lie
on the bed and I
feel
myself
slipping
slipping into hypatia's flayed and discarded skin he
lies
on his back he stares
up
through the ceiling small
elliptical
pillars pale pillars of light emanate from his eyes he
tells me
he's sleeping
the briefcase sits in the corner it thrums a low

thrum if you listen it
cannot
be heard a low electrical hum inside the briefcase
papers are moving a slow light succession of
shifting like dry leaves in the night
on weekends I try to discuss things things that I've
read and things that I've heard and he tells me about
abaca
do you know what abaca is?
it's a philippine plant the fibre of which is used in
the making of hemp
babbitt do you know about babbitt?
he does
he feels good about babbitt
buy babbitt! it's going to go up! babbitt is going to
go up!
babbitt? an alloy of tin, lead, copper, and antimoney
he's got holdings in babbitt
how do you spell universal inc?
ooo that's an interview question u n i
communications! that's how you spell it, television
radio film cables threading the the oceans
satellites filling the skies demonology! you wouldn't
believe the market in demons and if there is no
market create one! cause that's the way that we do
things! ethane formica gadolinium and the habile-
ment industry! husbandry, we're into that too
animals food we've all got to eat, fish! I don't care
for fish why don't I care? something about their
eyes, buy ironium! and judges! you never can tell
when you'll need one once I was in new zealand
inspecting a government site at night and a large
nocturnal parrot shit on my head I maintained
control of the situation by making an off the cuff
remark a play on words for I knew the name of
the parrot, kakapoo! that's what it's called!
I think on my feet and I love to read! I'm a patron
of the arts when I order a salad with nasturtium
seeds I pick them out I put em on the side of my
plate I'm afraid I'll choke on one and die I don't
see anything strange in that, do you?
afraid?
of capers?
no, love to caper but not in the city I live in the
price of oil will go up it's only a matter of time
you know I've always wanted a peke but I've always
bought a shepherd I don't feel any guilt about
that, do you know what raffia is? well don't buy

raffia stick with abaca! remember I told you that!
if I could get a decent instructor I know I could learn
to schuss, do you know the women's washroom?
well that's where my mother would take me until
I was nearly 6, for years I thought the uvula was
part of the female sex organ, it's not! it's that
fleshy thing that hangs down right in the back
of your throat, everyone has one, men and women!
government enterprises!
from wadis, to wall street we cover the waterfront!
that lost by a vote but I don't grieve it's all part
of the game

games aren't that important let bubu win tonight

zymosis?
he says nothing about zymosis
abattoir?
weaponry?
he says nothing about these things
I stare deep into his eyes trying to see who I
married
I fear for the children
the briefcase thrums in the corner
run away get away run! just one step then another
lift knees tendons run ligaments and bones just go
no
slowly walk slowly don't run I say just to the
ladies' they say right back no one around slow
freida speaks from behind me
slow measured pivot on right leg hip rotating in
socket right arm in graceful gesture followed by
left
push
freida
with her empty O mouth drifts down settles gently
into the concrete arms outstretched feet together

it's safe here

maybe I dreamt it

I would believe that I dreamt it
except
for the stain on my skirt which is probably
something I've spilt which is probably
we!
have a house in the country

I
of course
have not seen it but my grandfather has described
it to me many times my grandfather
raised his family in that house and so
did his father and
my brother used to say he thought he could
remember it from when he was a child the house
has beautiful arched windows and
big purple flowers grow under the windows and
there is a yard and inside
the rooms are fairly big and my grandmother
would keep them very clean I have a dream
sometimes
I am walking down the street in my dream and I see
our house it is as beautiful as my grandfather says
it is, it is a little smaller than I expect but the
flowers are there
and the windows
and then
I see
a boy playing in the yard and in my dream
I call to him
boy!
I say to him
whose house is that? and the boy says it is his
house and
I say
it is not your house! do you understand boy!
it is not your house!
and in my dream
the boy starts to cry and I understand that he is
afraid
and I am afraid
and I know that something has gone very wrong
sometimes in my dream the flowers
are a deep dark purple they look
like the blotches of blood on the whitewashed wall
where
the soldiers lined the young men up and beat them
and shot them I hid but my brother was very brave
and my mother was brave too for she held the flag
up even though it was forbidden she didn't do it for
the flag she did it for my brother!
sometimes in my dream when
I cry out it is not your house it is not your house
boy! we are surrounded by people they
stare at us

the boy and me
and we implore them to help us our lips
move but
no sound comes out at
least
they do not seem to hear us
they look at us and our lips move but they hear
nothing they
hear
nothing they say
my dream is a dream all a dream my house is green
shutters and shade says freida in white sweet
berries and bark is that true?
think about it
get it straight
no no wherever there be roof tarp cardboard on
hot air vent tree stone sand leafgrey dirtdark
or shimmering that is our house believe and act
on that belief!
I am afraid for the children
where are they?
they
are
playing I send a cheque to foster parents plan and
they send information on geography living conditions
and climate along with a snapshot he deducts it
from the income tax we go to a show although it's
hard to get tickets the briefcase
stays home they sing and we clap

(sings) he used to be a manly kinda man
in the locker room he'd always been a hit
he had push and punch and power
in committee they'd all cower
when he made a move to stand they'd quickly sit

he played a lotta poker in his time
he'll vote a tory ticket all his life
he likes tits and ass and whiskey
and he'd get a little frisky
when he went to those conventions *sans* the wife

(speaks) sans means without   he got about   picked up
the odd french phrase and a little more
but that was before   now look at his hands
they're shakin'   just feel his pulse
it's racin'

(sings) gone gone all of it's gone
his push and his punch and his power
now his masculine part don't work worth a fart
he's gotta stand tall but he can't fake it all
a woman has stolen his balls
   they can take a small rod
   it all sounds very odd

(speaks) I try holding the world and this in my head at the
same time

     Attempted song, more of a chant.

did!
not!
appear to be creatures of this world!
deep!
dark!
purple like blotches of blood on the wall!
real!
sharp!
abalone shells for skinning alive!

(speaks) he
hears nothing
I
lie in bed
the briefcase
thrums   I hear the wings of insects out in the hall
he pretends to sleep the hottish bodies of the
children move between cool sheets
I do not get up!
this is the way it is getting it straight it goes like
this
a mighty volcano erupts! he bursts into the bar both
his guns blazing! he paces! like a lion on the central
plains of africa like a raging bull he wheels in the
ring and the hot spanish sun beats on his back like
a nuclear sub that cuts through the frigid waters of
the polar sea in the arctic night like a million
megaton bomb boom fall in the ditch!
it goes
like this
people
die
people die
of kidney failure at the general
a light winks out

a black stick child eyes lightly glazed and flies
around her mouth a light winks out brown-skinned
boy falls backward scarlett blossoms stitched
across his shirt a light winks out so
so people die
they say it's in our nature
these things happen
what if
a million hiroshima bombs light up the sky
a billion viruses consort in pink moist passages why
then
if there be gods they'll
sit
on jupiter with weenie sticks and toast marshmallows
and when the dying coal that once was earth winks
out they'll
trundle off to take their rest on
orion
like boy scouts retiring to their tent
and if
they whisper in the night as boy scouts tend to do
in tents before they sleep
an epitaph for earth will ripple out like those
concentric circles from little stones my father
tossed in pools too deep to fish for fear of what
he'd catch
earth's undulating epitaph
They Died like Men!

this does not satisfy

they say I have a great imagination they
say
what are you thinking?
I say I asked him that!
I say I thought inside his head was a cornucopia
of rich and vivid images precise perceptive thought
I say what are you thinking?
I say have the courage to fear
I say the more boundless the deed the smaller the
hindrance
I say reality is surpassing imagination
I do not say I opened his briefcase
he says nothing
I say what are you thinking!
he says, nothing
I see he's right
inside his head they dropped the bomb it wasted all

the people but it kept the real estate
they say who dropped the bomb?
I say his parents
myrna says don't tell them that!
I say it's just a metaphor! what are you thinking!?

I
think
nothing
I
see
impressed in ash 4 million years ago a footprint in
moon dust on the dry sea of tranquility
a lunar print
they say
what are you thinking? I say how many steps is
that? I say one step! I say did it take 4 million
years to take that step or just a blink in time?
I say a blink! and I can travel faster further I've
done it anybody can but then I find it's always here
and now but that's not necessarily bad I say
they take away the national geographics and
the omni magazine
I don't care
It's all my fault says myrna myrna always lies
that's what I like about her it makes conversation so
easy
we skitter over the top of things like waterbugs
the television glows in its wire cage its voice
silenced by freida
ghosts dance across the surface of the screen
which is convex and rigid like the lens of myrna's
eyes she holds her hands over her ears so she can
hear
what's that? she says
it's a car
what's that? she says
it's a child
what's that? she says
it's a car bumper
what're they doin'? she says
they're tying the child to the car's bumper
your child?
no not my child my neighbour's child
what's that?
my neighbour's car with my child tied to its bumper
what's he sayin'?
instead of confusin' all you good people with a lot

a military and scientific jargon perhaps a simple
demonstration of the premise behind the policy of
nuclear deterrence would set your minds at ease
traffic accidents!
we all know about em' don't we folks
now suppose you could deter your neighbour from
runnin' into you on the road by seizing his children
and tyin' them to the front bumper of your car
suppose everyone were to do likewise
it's clearly evident accidents would decrease
indeed the chances of a single child dyin' on a car
bumper would be slight
perhaps by a miracle no child would die
in any event we can predict with absolute certainty
that on balance more lives would be saved than lost
and that's what nuclear deterrence is all about, folks
so when you hear balance of power holds innocent
hostage I want you to think
road safety and children!
myrna and I stare at the opaque convex eye hung
high in the corner
it stares back
it says nothing
faint grey forms shift in an off-white world
silence
what's that says myrna
uniforms
what's that?
flags
what's that?
fists
marching feet
martial music
tanks and missiles on parade
warheads
feed the hungry
silos
seed the skies with death
state
state

(sings) our state may be prey to terror and tears
rivers of blood may flow
heavens may rain both fire and flame
return the same   rules of the game
for fatherland motherland homeland
we have the right to die
we love our land   we'll make a stand

nation is all
the state will not fall

Less song, more frantic.

let women wail
power prevails
won't profits fall
make conference call
get credit line
meeting at nine
grabbing a cab
catching a light

Growing garbled.

corporate might
banking a sum
get to the top
ain't gonna stop ain't gonna stop aintgonnastop
ain'tgonna they
say
manic myrna says they say as she sits
by the desk on the floor with
her hands over her ears
in order to hear!
they say I say boom fall in a ditch!
I say ollie ollie oxen all outs in free
they say do you know why you're here?
I say
I'm waiting for someone to run home
last one home free frees the bunch
isn't that right? I say
I look for freida this is a face I remember
freida says I'm not mad I have a chemical imbalance
I'm not mad I have a chemical imbalance
compared to what?
I do not speak of the briefcase I say
I am guilty this is something I accept
they say
guilty of what?
I say nothing
freida thinks she knows freida knows
nothing myrna
says freida
is flat like a
super thin george
jensen watch in

profile she almost disappears casts only a
sliver of a shadow myrna says check it out flat
and thin circle
round I
see freida flat and thin inside her gold
george jensen cookie head are gently whirling cogs
and wheels if you
could pry the face off all
is still and
flat
im-pen-etrable which
is
what surprised
me
so her drifting down like some snow angel?
no
but
her george jensen head settles
into concrete the
space age
sealant
ruptured on this watch face no wheels and cogs
spill out no
microscopic quartz rolls like a fairy penny from her
ear
no
that's what drew me to her
she wasn't what she seemed to be   myrna
myrna!
myrna isn't here
myrna may be here
myrna says
get it straight myrna says
they
have
push and punch and power myrna
says
he
likes tits and ass and whiskey
I say
when
he gets
out of the shower
his penis looks like a snail that's
lost its shell
myrna laughs
although it is a sad thing
I don't tell him that

what are you thinking?
I say nothing
he accepts that
he doesn't know that I lie
I tell him nothing
lying beside him in bed I understand
there are things he does not want to be told
I tell him everything!

he says he is sleeping
I blame him
once I have opened his briefcase he cannot
plead
innocence
he invites people over
we sit in the den
he talks about buns
everyone laughs
this is a joke I think
the house settles a
fingernail scratches on glass outside
the window a tall woman in a yellow sari holds in
one hand a black and white photograph of a child
her other hand is empty I
make coffee I
check
on the children I am
watchful
I am
not
mad
I am
getting it straight
I am
aware
of the briefcase
I
have
the courage to fear inside
the briefcase is a reality surpassing
imagination at
night it thrums awaiting
release I
look
to the past for guidance I say
little boy little boy fat man?
I say little boy little boy fat man?
myrna says

can you fold a thousand cranes?
paper cranes?
folded paper cranes cry
spare me fat man can
we fold a thousand paper cranes folded paper cranes
cry spare us fat man cry little boy little boy cry
little boy cry little boy littleboyenolagayfatman! I!
say!
I say!
I fear!
I cannot!
fold!
a thousand paper cranes I say! Myrna says go back
to bed
I say
when sons and daughters die, their eyes closing on
rifle butt and boot, can they find home from there?
I say, when children die in dusty fields and streets,
is there no shadow cast across the painted blue that
shimmers from the swimming pool?
I say where are the children's graves? those whose
sin it was to be conceived of parents who once lived
where their parents lived?
myrna says
look
and
I
see
one of those towns on a river
a small little town on a river small little town train
running through and one of those squares in the
middle square little square in the middle a bite
in the air we walk
to the square my mother my brother and me
it is large and I look up I am small and looking up
old
men marching mothers' tears I am little looking up
wear a poppy hide the grief watch a general lay the
wreath place my hand against the stone
granite grey
mitten sticks
trace the letters carved in stone
here's to those
who lost their lives
and the finger
in mitten
rough woolen mitten
traces alphabet letters in stone I see old very old on

a delta by the sea many bridges over water and the
sky always blue
like a bowl
bebe cries mama laughs and the finger in mitten
rough woolen mitten traces alphabet letters in
stone gathering of people where paths cross yellow
skin and eyes we find strange they bleed weep when
children die lift their heads hope for something better
and the finger in mitten rough woolen mitten traces
alphabet letters in stone this does not satisfy!

faces press against the glass
the briefcase thrums
the children twist and turn their sheets uprooted
wrapt round them like a shroud
he lies on the bed his eyes gleam through
translucent lids I say myrna!
myrna isn't here
I say myrna?
listen to me myrna there

will be

no
more
alphabet letters in stone for

you and

I
will   will   will
spin
a   a
gossamer
net
of
of what
of women's hands and
and   rapunzel's hair and
that net
will encircle the globe and and
if a person stood
on on the far   left star of of
the utmost edge of of
cassiopeia's chair!
that net will
twinkle in the in the
inky cosmos like like fairy lights on a

on a christmas
tree and
what what what will it
spell?
myrna smiles
love myrna
myrna laughs
myrna moves her hips like a dog mounting my leg I
hit myrna! grab her hair! smash her face into the
floor! smash her face! smash! smash! smash!
smash!

I weep
privileges are suspended
freida takes me for stitches

I
I sit
in the kitchen I notice the sides of the briefcase
are bulged slightly like the pod of some alien plant
inside the contents ready themselves for birth I
note
it is locked
he carries the key
he will open it and it thrums secure in the
knowledge
I fear for the children
I am watched by those at the window
he is no longer him
I assemble
ingredients and utensils my
hands
carry out their task but I
am dead I am
down
and out and
down and
out
a secret is revealed to me I think
my hands are empty and in my chest a black hole
sucks my heart away and then
I hear
a voice and
in my hand I see I hold the key of truth and
in my breath a crimson throbbing grows and
I look up
I see the blue
I see

we are living
inside an egg and I
I see that it's blue
and the egg opens up
and a bright light
like a thousand suns and if I can open my eyes
just a little open my mind just a little try to
listen a little
listen
listen

Repeating what she hears.

the visible world   is no longer real
it's shattered   and turned into glass
a mirror   of ugliness   agony   shame
you know the way   you know the way to change
to change all of that the unseen world
is no longer a dream   it's   floating   just within
grasp a   shimmering radiant   heavenly   orb you
    know the way to   move yes move   towards
that
he shifts in the bed
I listen
I say
help me
I say
I know what's on your mind
because
I can read minds yes I see the words floating in the
air like paper darts ping ping and the words say
tell me ping
tell me
I want to believe I want to act but it's hard ping
it's an act of faith piiing
you've got to feel the blue piiiing
you've got to smell the light piiing
you've got to see the egg piiing
then our paper darts
will ride the electronic sea bounce round our island
universe   kiss the outer reaches of the milky way
and head for homes where others sit and watch
ping! listen ping! read our words hear our thoughts
ping!
the milky way I hear you say, now where's the blue
in that?
I'll tell you where
on the retina of each and every eye floats an image

of blue an oval of blue for we are living inside of
blue
inside of egg and it's blue
inside of egg that never contains inside of egg that
encloses and now I feel this shout and a paper dart
as big and luminous as a crescent moon impinges
upon my vision and that pale crescent shining shouts
now
black and white photos of children are pressed to
the windows I am watched
I open the drawer I would prefer some other way but
the house holds nothing useful for this I am
prepared
for this guilt I am not
prepared for the guilt of
doing
nothing
I walk up the stairs all sound ceases I have
entered some space between seconds air sacs of
lungs hang in suspension the prophetic bedclothes of
the children exude a pale lemon light I feel
purpose and peace and direction
he lies on his bed on his back,
I study him for an eon of time between seconds of
time
I see no one I know.
I
drive down
his lids flutter like a butterfly kiss and they open
he stares up into my face
he knows me.

yes
I am guilty of that
they say of what?

I let the briefcase hang from my hand as I walk to
the water I sit on the shore I use the key I tear
the papers to pieces I chew and I swallow the
disemboweled briefcase sits open and empty beside
me
I wait

maybe I dreamt it
myrna says they say I dreamt it
I say no
no
I say strike out strike down I say this is a lesser

crime I am guilty of that I accept that I hope I
have killed him, to have known and done
nothing? that is the crime of that I am not guilty
not guilty of that!

This is the egg talkin' to all members a the female
sex whether you be operatin' in a corporate world
surrounded by the pressures of the 8 to 4 the 9 to
5 swing shift night shift day shift not forgettin'
those with ambition and drive who aspire to
executive positions slave to the 13 and one-half
hour day I'm talkin' to you!
I'm includin' in this call for action all women who toil
in the home the field the factory on and offa the
street in and outa the jungle every race colour
and creed first second and third world under or
over on top or on bottom the egg is talkin' it's
talkin' to you!
What're you gonna do?

I say
go to the ladies
go beneath
go under
you'll find others there
I do have this stain on my skirt
but myrna will answer twice on the bus while
you
and I
spin a gossamer net of women's hands and rapunzel's
hair and that net will encircle the globe and if a
person stood on the far left star of the utmost
edge of cassiopeia's chair that net would twinkle
in the inky cosmos like fairy lights on a christmas
tree – and what would it spell?

what would it spell?

what would it spell?

The end.